W9-DDW-237

GREYSTONE'S

Creative Hands

EDITOR

Beverley Hilton

GREYSTONE PRESS/NEW YORK · TORONTO · LONDON

Volume 21

Contents

© Fratelli Fabri Editore, Milan 1966, 1967
Marshall Cavendish Limited 1970, 1971, 1972, 1973, 1975
Manufactured in the United States of America
Library of Congress Catalog Card No. 75-8338

Much of the material contained herein has
previously been published in separate parts
under the title Golden Hands.

BAZAAR

Flower-filled gifts

Make several of these fragrant lavender balls as gifts for your friends or as bazaar items. Each one can be made quite unique by varying the fabrics and embroidery stitches.

You will need:
☐ thin cardboard for the 12 templates
☐ scraps of four kinds of fabric
☐ 4 inches of ribbon or cord
☐ lavender

To make the patches
Cut out 12 cardboard templates from the tracing pattern given. Be careful to trace and cut out the shapes accurately or the patches will not match together. Cut out 12 pieces of material, three shapes from each of the four fabrics, making each piece a little larger than the card shapes. The fabric should be quite sturdy and of close weave – cottons are ideal – and all four should be of similar weight. Pin a cardboard shape onto the center of each piece of fabric on the wrong side (Figure 1). Fold the edges of the material over the cardboard and baste down (Figure 2), making the corners neat. Remove pins.

To make the ball
Join the patches by placing two together, right sides facing, and overcasting one edge with tiny stitches (Figure 3). Using Figure 4 as an assembly guide, join four shapes around the central patch for one side and repeat with the other six shapes for the second side. Join the two sides together, leaving two seams unstitched. Remove the basting stitches and the cardboards, trim any excess fabric, and turn to the right side. Fill ball with lavender and neatly overcast the last two seams, inserting the looped cord or ribbon in one corner before closing it up. Choose embroidery floss to tone with the fabrics and, working with two strands, decorate the sides of the ball with straight stitch flowers, French knots, double cross-stitch or any other suitable design.

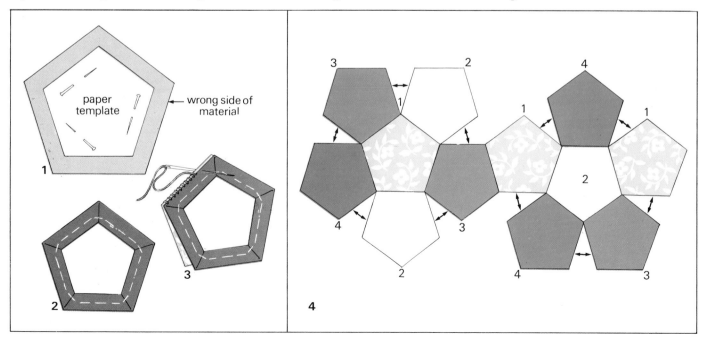

TOYS

A patchwork dog

This colorful, soft patchwork dog is easy to sew, and makes an engaging toy for small children. Made up in bright cotton fabrics, Patch is the perfect way to use up left-over scraps of material.

You will need:
- [ ] 1 yard cotton fabric, or scraps of different colored fabrics
- [ ] small bag of kapok
- [ ] 2 black buttons, for eyes
- [ ] black sports yarn
- [ ] 8 inches of ribbon
- [ ] small bell

To make the dog
Draw up the pattern pieces from the graph given here. $\frac{1}{2}$ inch seam allowance is included throughout.

Cut one piece A, then reverse the pattern piece to cut the second. Repeat with pattern piece B, using contrasting fabric if desired. Cut one piece C, using a third contrasting fabric if desired.

With right sides together, join pieces A and B along the dotted line. Repeat for the second side of the dog.

With right sides together, join the two halves of the dog along the dotted line between points X and Y.

Pin out the upper body with right side uppermost, and place piece C on top, right side down.

Matching up leg pieces all around, and working away from point Y, baste and stitch all around the under body, legs and feet (Fig. 1) to join the under part of the dog to the upper body. Leave a small length of seam open for turning and stuffing. Turn the dog right side out. Stuff the body of the dog firmly with kapok. Overcast the seam to close.

Using pattern piece D, cut out four ears from contrasting fabrics, reversing the pattern piece for the second pair. With right sides together, sew each pair of ear shapes together, leaving the straight edges open. Turn right side out.

Turn in the raw edges of the ears and stitch together, taking a $\frac{1}{4}$ inch tuck at right angles to the center of the seam (Fig. 2). Stitch the ears to the sides of the head. The tucks hold the ears slightly away from the side of the head.

Stitch the buttons in position to form the eyes, and use the black yarn to work a nose in satin stitch and a mouth in chain stitch (Fig. 3).

Stitch the ribbon around the neck of the dog to form a collar, and stitch the bell to the front of the ribbon.

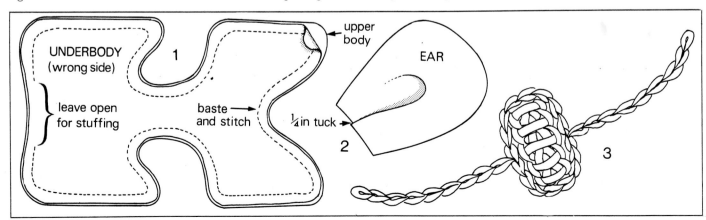

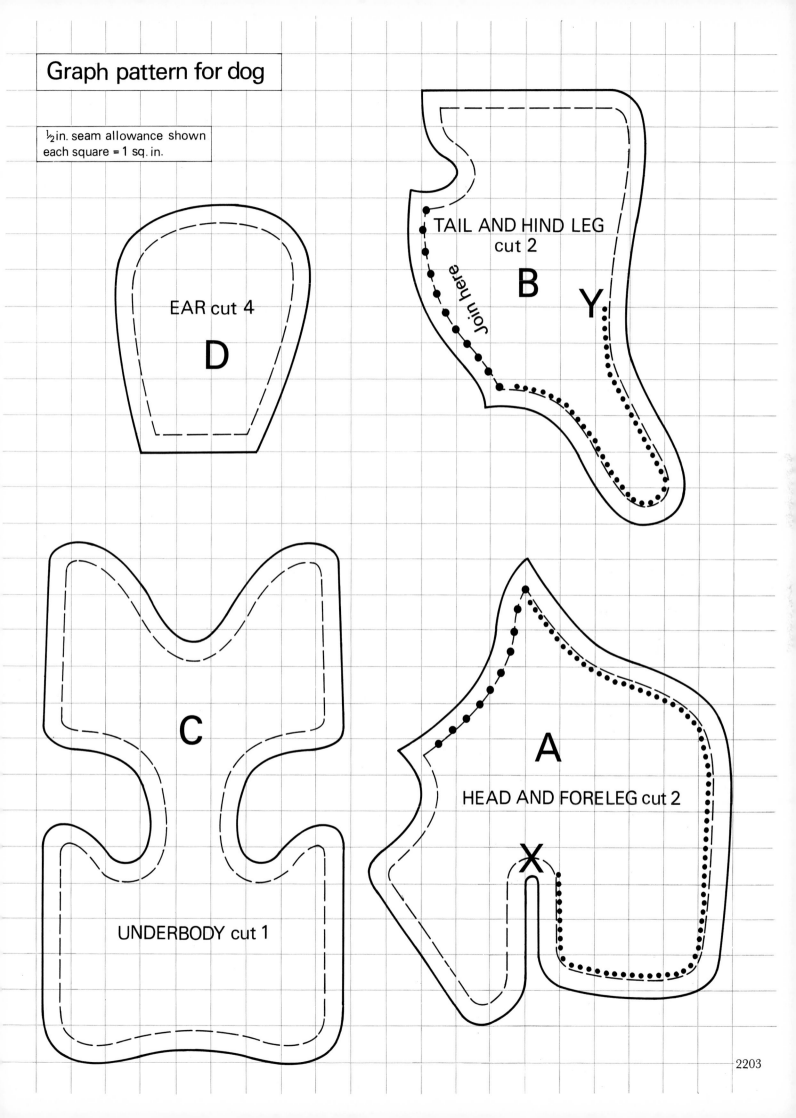

Graph pattern for dog

½ in. seam allowance shown
each square = 1 sq. in.

EAR cut 4
D

TAIL AND HIND LEG
cut 2
B   Y

Join here

C

UNDERBODY cut 1

A

HEAD AND FORELEG cut 2

X

2203

Trim tunic

This neat tunic dress for a little girl is elasticized at the waist and wrist for ease of movement, zip-fronted and finished with roomy patch pockets. It can be worn as a dress or as a tunic over pants, or teamed with a chunky sweater and colored tights.

Fabrics and notions

- ☐ 54 inch wide fabric with or without nap, both sizes, $1\frac{1}{3}$ yards, or
- ☐ 36 inch wide fabric without nap, both sizes, $1\frac{3}{4}$ yards
- ☐ gathering elastic 2 inches wide, size 6, 14 inches; size 8, $15\frac{1}{2}$ inches
- ☐ $\frac{1}{4}$ inch wide elastic, both sizes, $\frac{3}{8}$ yard
- ☐ zipper, size 6, 14 inches; size 8, 16 inches
- ☐ 2 $\frac{3}{4}$-inch buttons
- ☐ sewing thread to match fabric
- ☐ graph paper for patterns

The pattern

This pattern is to fit a 6 or 8 year old with a chest measurement of 28 inches for size 6, and 30 inches for size 8.

Draw up the pattern pieces from the graph given here, in which one square represents one inch square. No seam or hem allowance has been included on the pattern, so add $\frac{5}{8}$ inch to all seam edges and $1\frac{1}{2}$ inches to sleeve and hem edges.

Making the tunic

1. With right sides together, baste and stitch the dress fronts to the dress back at the side seams. Press the seams open.

2. Position the gathering elastic along the lines indicated on the pattern. Pin the elastic down and machine stitch along the length of the elastic at intervals of $\frac{3}{8}$ inch.

3. With right sides together, baste and stitch the center front seam from the circle to the hem. Press seam open. Turn the seam allowance on the center front opening to the wrong side. Baste and press.

Insert the zipper following the instructions given on the package.

4. With right sides together, baste and stitch the fronts to the back at the shoulder seam. Press seam open.

5. With right sides together, join the front neck facings to the back neck facing at the shoulder seam. Press the seam open.

6. With right sides together, matching

center back, center front and shoulder seams, baste and stitch the neck facing to the dress. Press the seam toward the facing and clip the curves where necessary. On the right side of the facing, top-stitch $\frac{1}{8}$ inch away from the seam. Trim away excess seam allowance. Turn the facing to the wrong side of the dress, and, on the right side, baste around the neckline, easing it into shape.

7. Turn under the facing seam allowance at the center fronts and slip-stitch to the zipper tape. Catch the facing to the dress at the shoulder seams. Press on the wrong side.

8. With right sides together, baste and stitch around the pocket and pocket facing, leaving a gap to turn the pocket. Clip across the corners, on curves and trim back excess seam allowance.

9. Turn the pocket right side out. Baste around the edge, easing the pocket into shape. Slip-stitch the opening to close and press flat on the wrong side.

10. Place the pocket in the position indicated on the pattern. Baste and top-stitch the pocket to the dress $\frac{1}{4}$ inch away from pocket edge. Slip-stitch the top-stitched edge of the pocket to the dress. Press on wrong side.

11. With right sides together, baste and stitch the sleeve seam. Press the seam open.

12. With right sides together, matching notches, underarm seam to side seam and circle to shoulder seam, baste and stitch the sleeve into the armhole with the sleeve uppermost.

13. Turn up the sleeve hem. Baste and top-stitch $\frac{3}{8}$ inch from the folded edge, leaving an opening for inserting the elastic. Cut a length of elastic to the measurement of the wrist, plus $\frac{3}{4}$ inch. Thread the elastic through the sleeve hem and stitch the ends of the elastic together to secure. Close the opening and catch the sleeve hem to the sleeve with invisible hemming.

14. Try on the dress and mark the hem line. Turn up the hem and baste along the fold. Trim the hem allowance to an even depth all around and stitch the hem to the dress using invisible hemming. Press.

15. With right sides together, baste and stitch the tab and the tab facing, leaving a small opening for turning. Snip across the corners and trim excess seam allowance. Turn the tab right side out. Baste all around the edge easing the tab into shape. Slip-stitch the opening to close. Press flat on the wrong side. Top-stitch all around $\frac{1}{4}$ inch from edge.

16. Work two buttonholes by hand or machine at the positions indicated on the pattern.

17. Sew buttons to the positions shown.

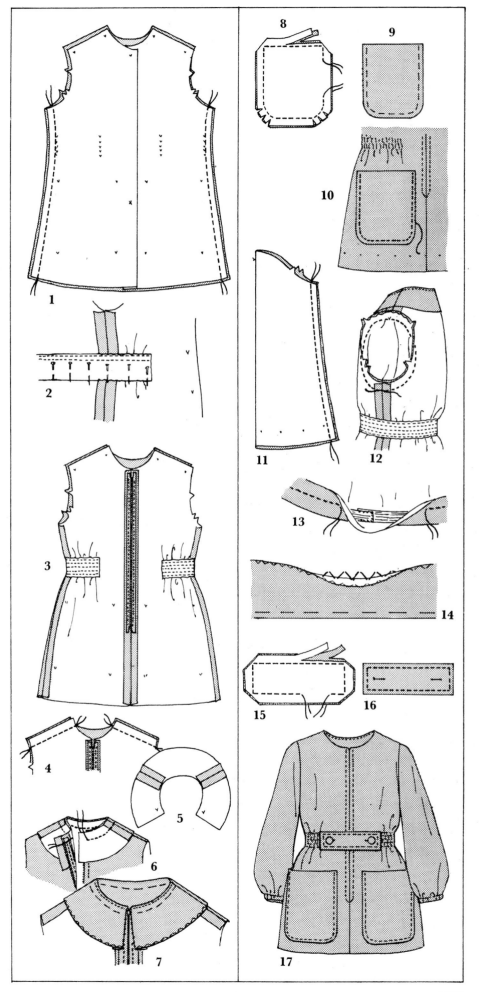

Graph pattern for child's tunic

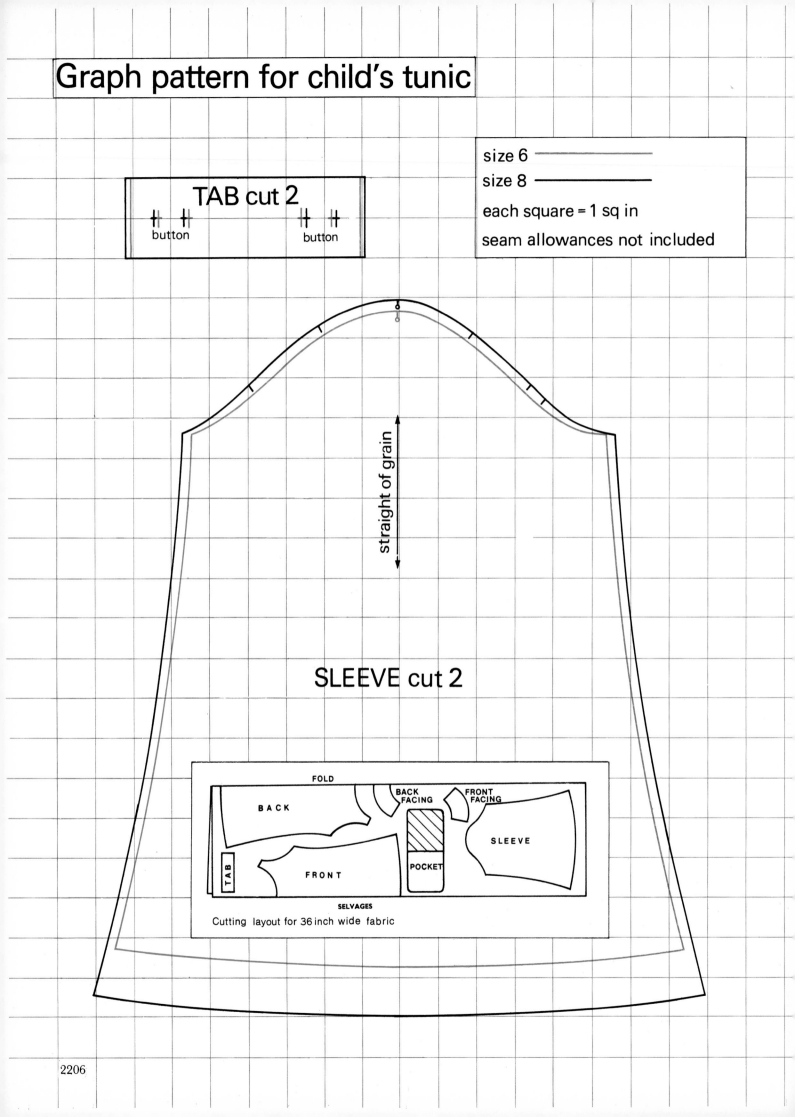

TAB cut 2

button   button

size 6 ————
size 8 ————
each square = 1 sq in
seam allowances not included

straight of grain

SLEEVE cut 2

FOLD

BACK

BACK FACING

FRONT FACING

TAB

FRONT

POCKET

SLEEVE

SELVAGES

Cutting layout for 36 inch wide fabric

2206

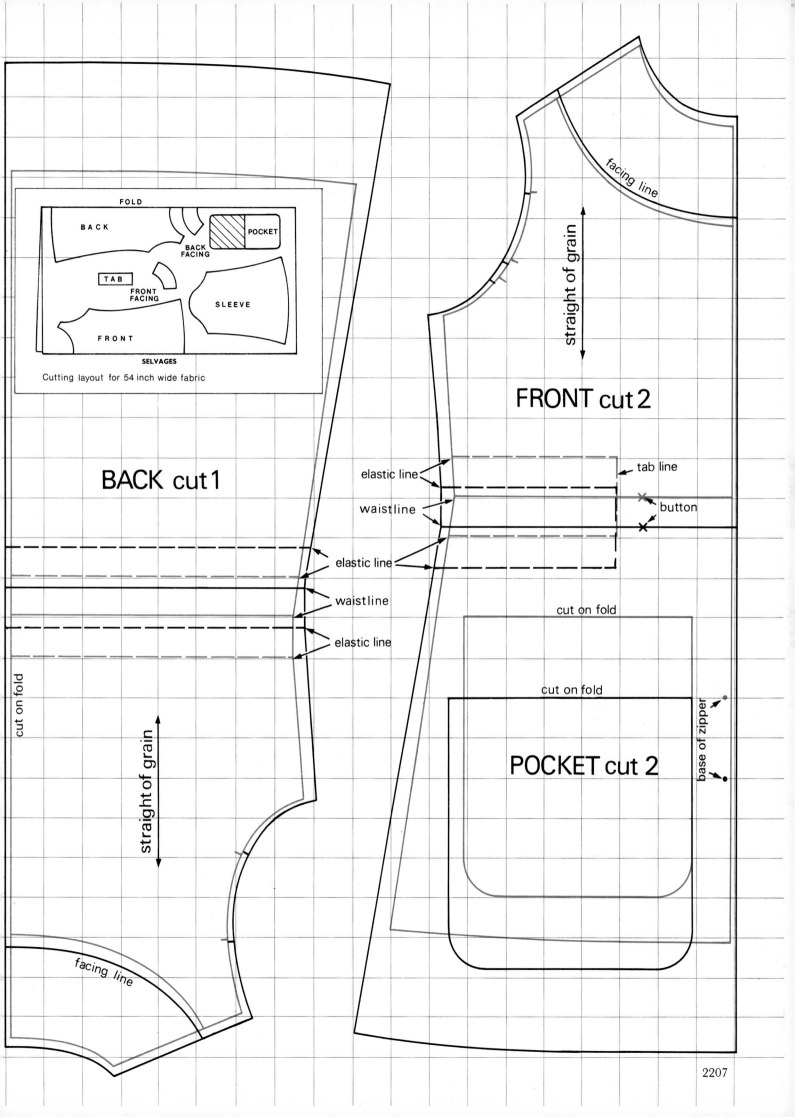

FOLD

BACK

POCKET

BACK
FACING

TAB

FRONT
FACING

SLEEVE

FRONT

SELVAGES

Cutting layout for 54 inch wide fabric

BACK cut 1

FRONT cut 2

facing line

straight of grain

elastic line

tab line

waistline

button

elastic line

elastic line

waistline

cut on fold

elastic line

cut on fold

cut on fold

POCKET cut 2

base of zipper

cut on fold

straight of grain

facing line

2207

Checkmate

This elegant chessboard, edged with a classic Greek key motif, makes a handsome addition to any room. The stitchery might be placed under glass, as a protection against dust and dirt, to form an attractive and unusual table.

To make the chessboard

Materials required to make the chessboard measuring 21 inches by 21½ inches:

☐ Anchor Tapestry Yarn in the following colors and quantities:
15 skeins black 0403
12 skeins cream 0386
12 skeins Gobelin green 0861
2 skeins gray 0497

☐ ¾ yard double thread canvas (10 holes to the inch), 27 inches wide

☐ 2½ yards black cord, ¼ inch in diameter

☐ tapestry frame with 27 inch tapes

☐ backing board

☐ Scovill/Dritz tapestry needle No. 18

Alternative threads for the chessboard:

Method of working

Divide the canvas through the center both horizontally and vertically with a line of basting stitches run along a line of holes. Mount the canvas on the frame, with the tapes on the raw edges.

To work the design, follow the working chart which gives one quarter of the playing area of the chessboard and the border. Each background square represents the intersection of two double threads of the canvas, or one stitch.

The design is worked throughout in trammed tent stitch; the tramming acts as a padding for the tent stitch and helps to cover the canvas more completely. Begin working in the center of the design and work outward toward the border.

After the embroidery has been completed, place the backing board (heavy cardboard or hardboard) over the back of the work. Fold the surplus canvas to the back and secure by pinning into the edge of the board. Then lace horizontally and vertically across the back with a strong thread. Remove the pins and attach the cord to the outer edges.

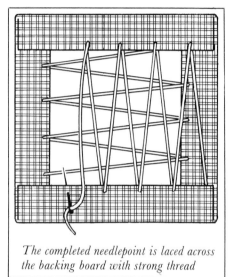

The completed needlepoint is laced across the backing board with strong thread

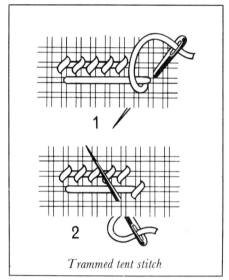

Trammed tent stitch

A detail of the chessboard showing one corner

☐ D.M.C. Matte Embroidery Cotton in each of the following colors and quantities:
23 skeins black 2310
18 skeins almond green 2469
18 skeins ecru
18 skeins gray 2415

☐ D.M.C. 6-Strand Floss in the following colors and quantities (use nine strands throughout):
40 skeins black 310
32 skeins almond green 3346
32 skeins ecru 437
32 skeins gray 415

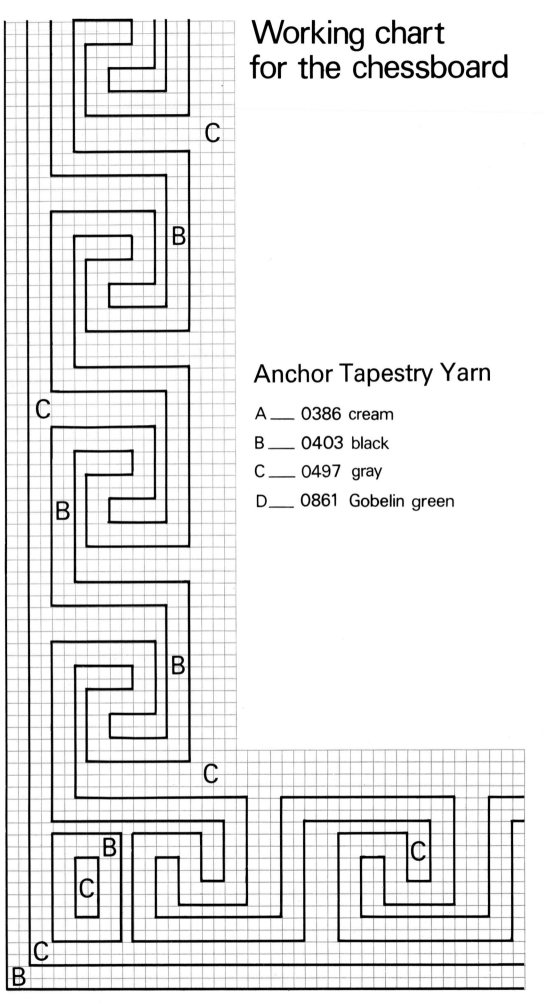

Working chart
for the chessboard

Anchor Tapestry Yarn

A ___ 0386 cream

B ___ 0403 black

C ___ 0497 gray

D ___ 0861 Gobelin green

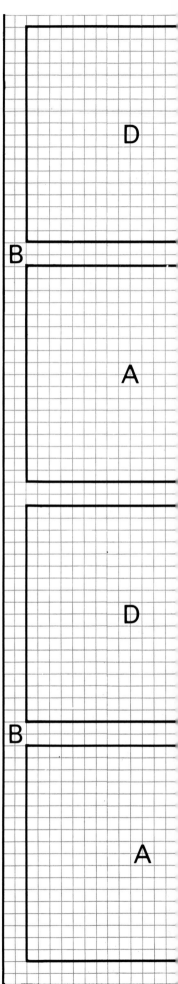

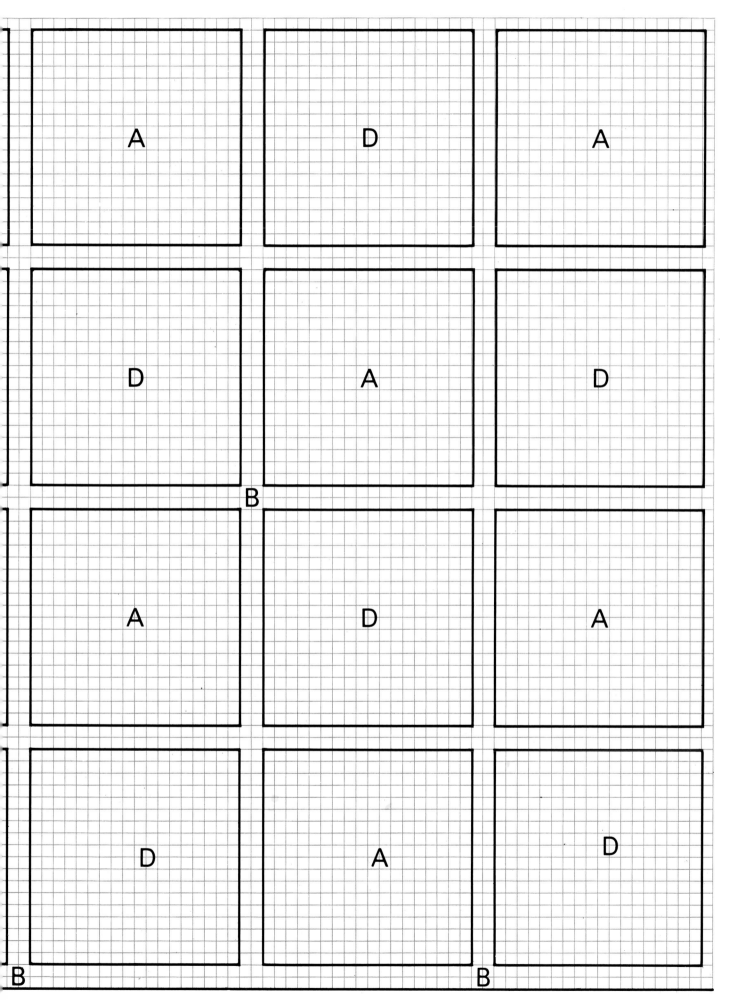

2211

Simple dress for sunny days

This pretty sundress is made in bright yellow gingham and the bodice is decorated with large, gaily colored daisies worked in simple stitches. For the embroidery instructions see Stitchery Ideas on page 2230.

Fabrics and notions

For this gingham sundress you will need:
- ☐ 36 inch wide fabric without nap, size 10, $4\frac{5}{8}$ yards; size 12, $4\frac{3}{4}$ yards; size 14, $4\frac{7}{8}$ yards; size 16, 5 yards
- ☐ 18 inch zipper
- ☐ sewing thread to match fabric
- ☐ graph paper for pattern

The pattern

The pattern given here is for sizes 10, 12, 14 and 16.

Draw up the pattern pieces to scale from the graph pattern. No seam allowances are included on the pattern, so add $\frac{5}{8}$ inch to all edges when cutting out the pattern pieces.

To make the sundress

1. On the front bodice, cut away the excess fabric inside the darts, leaving $\frac{5}{8}$ inch seam allowance.

2. With right sides together, baste and stitch the front darts. Clip on the curve where necessary. Press the darts away from the center front.

3. With right sides together, baste and stitch the back bodice darts. Press flat toward the center back.

4. With right sides together, baste and stitch the facings to the front and back bodice around the neckline and armholes, leaving $\frac{5}{8}$ inch free at the shoulder seams.

5. Turn the facings to the inside of the bodice and stitch the shoulder seams. Press the seams open.

6. Turn in the shoulder seam of the facings and slip stitch the seams to close.

7. With right sides together, join the shoulder seam of the flounce. Press the seam open. Along the curved edge of the flounce pieces, make an $\frac{1}{8}$ inch turning to the wrong side and top-stitch by

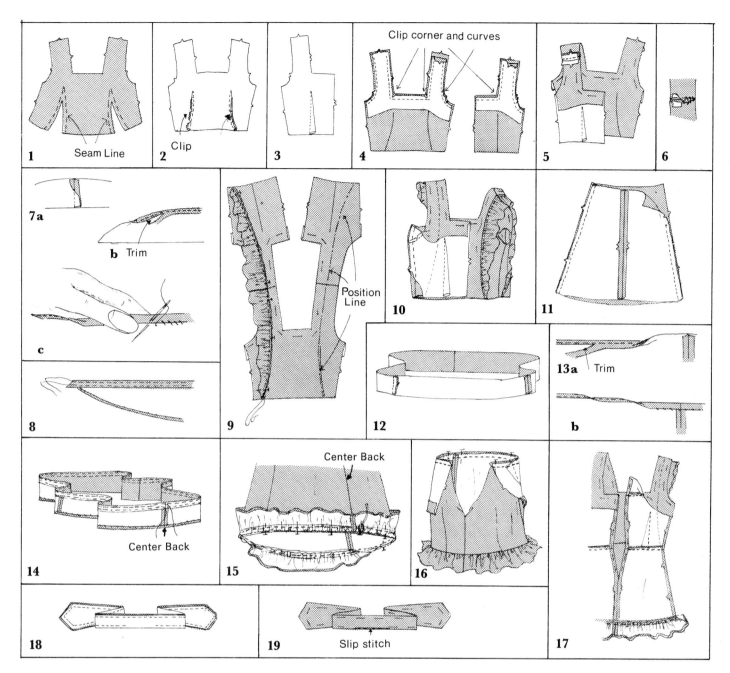

1 Seam Line

2 Clip

3

4 Clip corner and curves

5

6

7a

b Trim

c

8

9 Position Line

10

11

12

13a Trim

b

14 Center Back

15 Center Back

16

17

18

19 Slip stitch

machine. Press the stitched edge flat. Trim away any excess fabric close to the machine stitching. Turn a narrow hem and hem it by hand. Press the hem edge flat.

8. On the straight edge of the flounce, turn $\frac{5}{8}$ inch seam allowance to the wrong side and work two rows of gathering stitches along the edge.

9. Matching the center of the flounce to the shoulder seam, draw up the gathers to fit, and top-stitch the flounce to the line indicated on the pattern pieces.

10. With right sides together, baste and stitch the side and facing seams in one continuous line. Press the seams open. On the raw edge of the facing, turn $\frac{1}{8}$ inch to the wrong side and top-stitch by machine close to the edge. Press the stitched edge flat. Tack the underarm edge of the facing to the side seam.

11. With right sides together, baste and

stitch the side seams of the skirt. With right sides together, baste and stitch the center back seam, leaving open above the circle to insert the zipper. Press all seams open.

12. With right sides together, join the bias cut pieces for the skirt hem ruffle into a circle.

13. On one edge of the ruffle, turn under $\frac{1}{8}$ inch to the wrong side and top-stitch by machine. Press the hem edge flat. Trim away any excess fabric close to the machine line. Press flat. Turn a narrow hem and sew by hand. Press the hem flat.

14. Work two rows of gathering threads along the seam line around the un-hemmed edge of the ruffle.

15. With right sides together, pin the ruffle to the hem of the skirt, distributing the gathers evenly all around. Baste and stitch the ruffle to the skirt. Press the

seam toward the waistline.

16. With right sides together, matching side seams and center fronts, baste and stitch the skirt to the dress bodice. Press the seam up toward the bodice.

17. Turn and baste the center back opening seam allowance to the wrong side. Press flat.

Insert the zipper in the back opening, following the instructions given on the zipper package.

18. With right sides together, baste and stitch the belt facing to the belt, leaving a 4 inch opening at the center back to turn the belt right side out. Trim and grade the seams, cutting across the corners.

19. Turn the belt right side out. Baste all around the edge, easing the belt into a good shape.

Slip stitch the opening closed and press the belt flat.

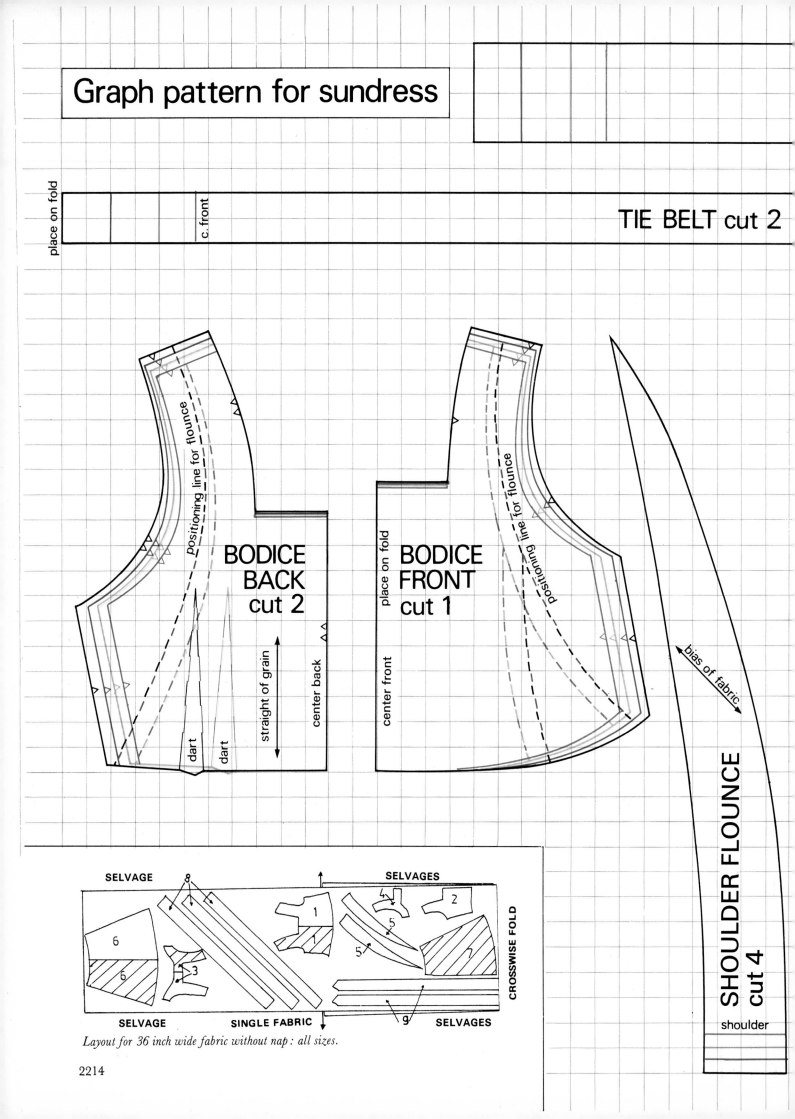

Graph pattern for sundress

place on fold

c. front

TIE BELT cut 2

BODICE BACK cut 2

Positioning line for flounce

straight of grain

center back

dart dart

place on fold

BODICE FRONT cut 1

center front

positioning line for flounce

positioning line for flounce

bias of fabric

SHOULDER FLOUNCE cut 4

shoulder

SELVAGE

8

SELVAGES

6

1

4

2

6

3

5

5

9

CROSSWISE FOLD

SELVAGE   SINGLE FABRIC   SELVAGES

Layout for 36 inch wide fabric without nap : all sizes.

2214

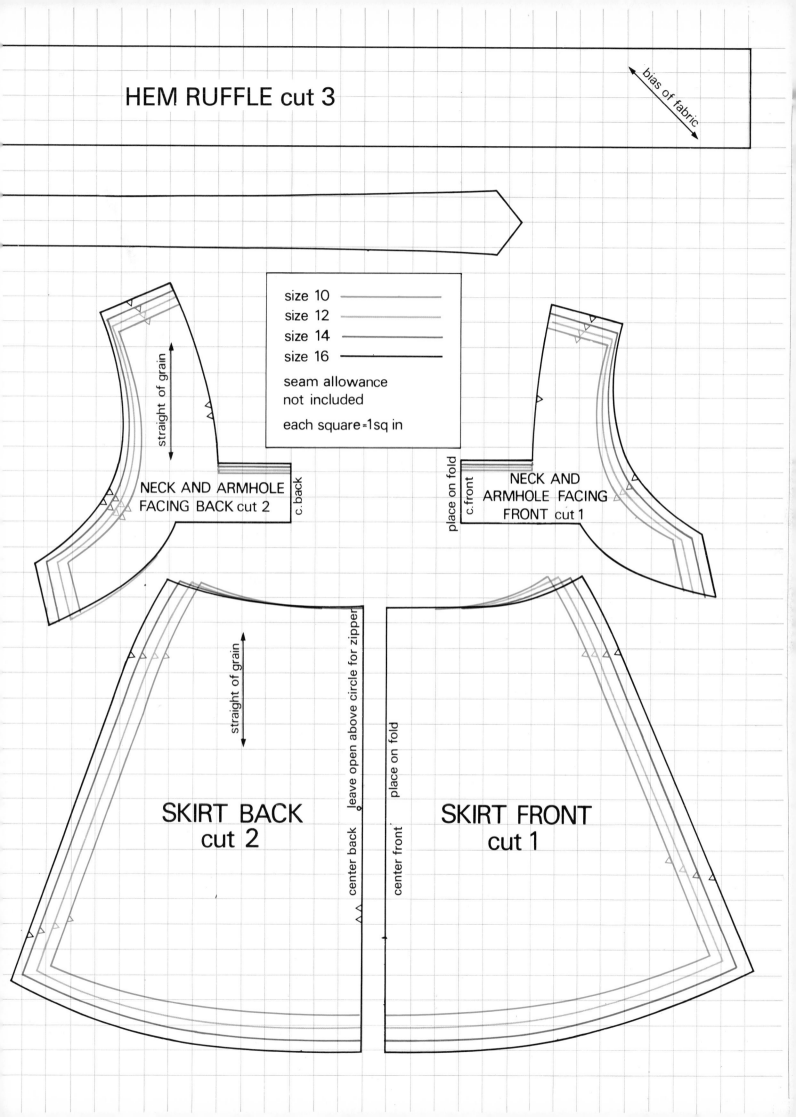

HEM RUFFLE cut 3

bias of fabric

size 10 ⎯⎯⎯⎯
size 12 ⎯⎯⎯⎯
size 14 ⎯⎯⎯⎯
size 16 ⎯⎯⎯⎯

seam allowance
not included

each square = 1 sq in

NECK AND ARMHOLE
FACING BACK cut 2

straight of grain

c. back

place on fold

c. front

NECK AND
ARMHOLE FACING
FRONT cut 1

SKIRT BACK
cut 2

straight of grain

center back

leave open above circle for zipper

center front

place on fold

SKIRT FRONT
cut 1

KNITTING FOR
THE FAMILY
Knitted
knee socks

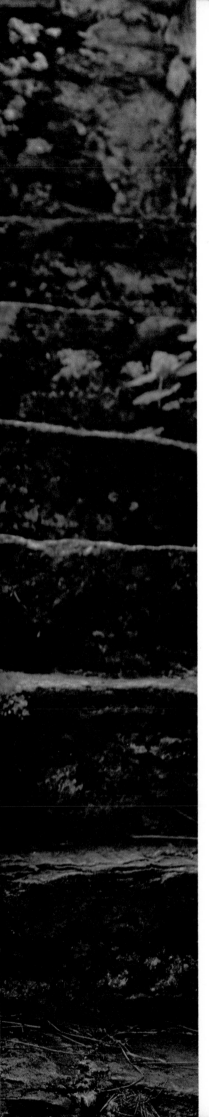

Whether you choose them plain or prefer a fancy version, these knee socks are worked on four needles, which means they give the smoothest fit.

Sizes

To fit foot 9[9½:10]in
Ribbed socks. Length from top of heel to top, 21in
Lacy socks. Length from top of heel to top, 23in

> **Gauge**
> 8 sts and 10 rows to 1in over rib patt on No. 3 needles

Materials

Spinnerin Sabrina
50 grm. balls
Ribbed socks. 5 balls
Lacy socks. 5 balls
One set of four No. 2 double-pointed needles (or Canadian No. 11)
One set of four No. 3 double-pointed needles (or Canadian No. 10)
Lacy socks only. One No. D (3.00 mm) crochet hook

Ribbed socks

Using set of four No. 2 needles, cast on 76 sts. Join. Work in rounds of K1, P1 rib for 4in, dec one st at end of last round. 75 sts.
Change to set of four No. 3 needles.
Next round P1, *K3, P2, rep from * to last 4 sts, K3, P1.
Rep last round until work measures 10½in from beg.
Next round P1, K2 tog, patt to last 3 sts, sl 1, K1, psso, P1.
Work 7 rounds rib as established.
Rep these 8 rounds once more.
Next round P1, P2 tog, patt to last 3 sts, P2 tog, P1.
Work 7 rounds rib as established.
Continue dec one st at each end of every 8th round until 55 sts rem.
Continue without shaping until work measures 21in from beg, ending at end of a round.

**Heel

Next round K13, sl last 13 sts of round onto this same needle and slip rem 29 sts on two needles for instep.

Continue on these 26 sts for 23 rows more, beg and ending with a P row.
Next row K16, K2 tog, K1, turn.
Next row Sl 1, P7, P2 tog, P1, turn.
Next row Sl 1, K8, K2 tog, K1, turn.
Next row Sl 1, P9, P2 tog, P1, turn.
Next row Sl 1, K10, K2 tog, turn.
Next row Sl 1, P10, P2 tog, turn.
Rep last two rows 4 times more. 12 sts.
Next row K6.
Slip instep sts onto one needle. Using the spare needle, K next 6 sts, pick up and K 12 sts along side of heel, using the next needle patt across 29 sts on holder, using 3rd needle, pick up and K 12 sts along side of heel and K rem 6 sts. 65 sts.
Next round On first and third needles work in st st, and on 3rd needle work in patt.
Next round On first needle K to last 2 sts, sl 1, K1, psso, on second needle rib to end, on third needle K2 tog, K to end.
Continue dec in this manner every 3rd round until 55 sts rem.
Continue without shaping until foot measures 7[7½:8]in from back of heel or 2in less than desired finished length, ending at end of a round.

Shape toe

Next round *K5, sl 1, K1, psso, rep from * to last 6 sts, K6. 48 sts.
Work 5 rounds st st.
Next round *K4, sl 1, K1, psso, rep from * to end. 40 sts.
Work 4 rounds st st.
Next round *K3, sl 1, K1, psso, rep from * to end. 40 sts.
Work 3 rounds st st.
Next round *K2, sl 1, K1, psso, rep from * to end. 24 sts.
Work 2 rounds st st.
Next round *K1, sl 1, K1, psso, rep from * to end. 16 sts.
Next round K.
Next round *Sl 1, K1, psso, rep from * to end. 8 sts.
Break off yarn. Using a darning needle, thread end through rem sts and fasten off.

Lacy socks

Using two of four No. 2 needles, cast on 77 sts. Do not join.
1st row K1, *P1, K1, rep from * to end.
2nd row P1, *K1, P1, rep from * to end.
Rep these 2 rows until work measures 3in, ending with a 2nd row.
Join into a round by K tog first and last sts and continue on four needles in K1, P1 rib until work measures 6in from beg, dec one st at end of last round.
N.B. Open part should be positioned at center front and the end of the round at center back. 75 sts.
Change to set of four No. 3 needles.
1st round P1, *K3, P2, rep from * to last 4 sts, K3, P1.
2nd round P1, (K3, P2) 6 times, K1, ytf, sl 1, K1, psso, P2, K3, P2, K2 tog, ytf, K1, (P2, K3) 6 times, P1.
3rd round As 1st.
4th round P1, (K3, P2) 6 times, K2 tog, ytf, K1, P2, K3, P2, K1, ytf, sl 1, K1, psso, (P2, K3) 6 times, P1.
Rep these 4 rounds until work measures 12½in from beg.
Next round P1, K2 tog, patt to last 3 sts, sl 1, K1, psso, P1.
Continue dec as given for Ribbed Socks at beg and end of every 8th round until 55 sts rem.
Continue without shaping until work measures 23in from beg, ending at the end of a round.
Keeping 3 sts at each side of center front 7 sts in patt throughout, continue as given for Ribbed Socks from ** to end.

Finishing

Press work under a damp cloth, using a cool iron only.
Lacy socks only. Using No. D hook, work one row sc around front opening at top of the sock.
Make a cord of chs and thread through edges of crochet to tie in a bow.

2218

Patchwork in silk

These beautiful silk pillows are an exquisite example of how patchwork can be worked to look both subtle and delicate. They are made up of traditional hexagonal shapes and the colors have been arranged to form a pattern of subtle pastel shades. Or, brightly colored patches can be arranged at random for a more modern look.

You will need:

- [ ] pillow forms
- [ ] large bag of silk fabric scraps in different plain colors
- [ ] silk fabric in a toning plain color to cover the pillow
- [ ] preshrunk piping cord
- [ ] stiff cardboard
- [ ] paper

It is important to select the colors for each pillow carefully. Use either three different colors in equal proportions, or four different colors, making one predominant, to tone with the color scheme of the room.

For a really elegant effect, select the silk fabric in shades that are close to each other in tone.

If using slubbed or grained silk, work the patches so that they lie with the grain running in opposite ways to reflect the light in different directions. This gives a most attractive and unusual effect.

To make the patches

The fabric shapes are cut out using a template, and then backed with paper to keep them firm while they are being stitched.

Templates can be made quite satisfactorily from stiff cardboard. To make patches the same size as those illustrated, trace off the hexagonal shape given here and cut it out from cardboard.

Make two templates, one exactly to the size given and the other ¼ inch larger all around. The smaller is for cutting the paper shapes, the larger for cutting the fabric pieces, with a seam allowance all around. The backing used for the patches should be of fairly stiff paper, to keep them firm in working. Magazine covers or old greeting cards are suitable for this.

To prepare the patches

Cut out paper and fabric shapes.

There are approximately 8–10 hexagons along each edge of the patchwork square, but this can be varied according to the size of the pillow.

It is advisable to work out both the size and the color arrangement beforehand on a sheet of graph paper. In this way it is possible to work out exactly how many shapes of each color are required, remembering that the template shape given here is the exact size of the finished patch.

Pin a paper shape to the wrong side of a fabric patch, placing the paper so that the turnings are exactly equal on all sides. Fold the turnings over the paper, pulling the fabric gently taut, and baste the fabric to the patch. Do not tie a knot in the thread, but simply baste the paper in place and remove the pins (Fig. 1).

Prepare the required number of patches in the same way.

Joining the patches

Patches can be joined by straight machine stitching (Fig. 2a) or by hand. To join patches by hand, place two backed patches together, right sides facing, with edges carefully matched. Overcast along one edge, using a fine needle and matching thread (Fig. 2b). Never pull an edge to fit if it does not match up, but rip the patch and begin again. When all the patches are stitched together, press the work lightly on the wrong side. Snip the basting threads, pull them out, then remove the paper backing.

To make the pillow

Make a piped pillow cover from plain silk fabric in one of the colors used to make the patchwork. Cover the pillow, and either slipstitch together the final seam or insert a zipper.

Lay the finished patchwork on one side of the pillow and sew neatly in place.

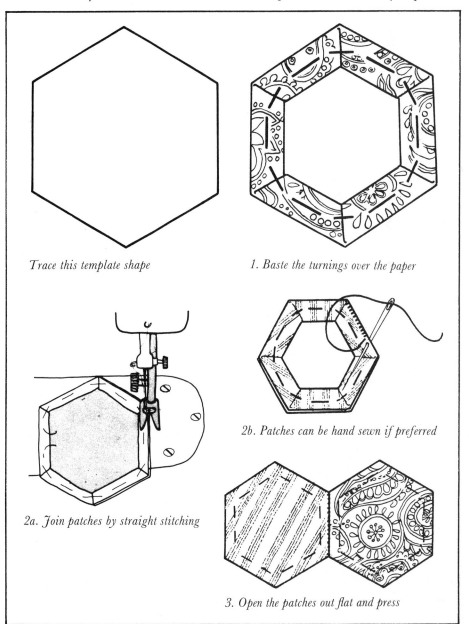

Trace this template shape

1. Baste the turnings over the paper

2a. Join patches by straight stitching

2b. Patches can be hand sewn if preferred

3. Open the patches out flat and press

Knit and crochet for the sun

Get ready for sunny days by
the sea by making a colorful striped bikini or an
elegant one-piece swimsuit.

Sizes
Knitted bikini. Directions
are for 32in bust
Crochet bikini. Directions
are for 34 to 36in bust
Swimsuit. Directions are
for 32 to 34in bust

Gauge
Knitted bikini and swimsuit.
8 sts and 11 rows to 1in over st st worked on No.2 needles
Crochet bikini. 27 sts and 15 rows to 4in over patt worked on No.D hook

Materials
Brunswick Fairhaven Fingering Yarn 1 oz. skeins
Knitted bikini. 2 skeins main color, A, white
1 skein each of contrasts B, C, D, E, green, yellow, blue and pink respectively
One pair No. 2 knitting needles (or Canadian No. 11)
One set of four No. 2 double-pointed needles
Waist length elastic
Crochet bikini. 4 skeins main color, A, blue
2 skeins contrast B, pink
One No. D (3.00 mm) crochet hook
Waist length elastic
Swimsuit. 6 skeins main color, A, white
1 skein each (or small amounts) of contrasts B, C, D, E, yellow, blue, green and red respectively
One pair No. 2 knitting needles (or Canadian No. 11)
One set of 4 No. 2 double-pointed needles

Knitted bikini pants back

Using No.2 straight needles and A, cast on 20 sts.

Work in st st, inc one st at each end of first and every other row until there are 66 sts, ending with a P row.
Cast on 2 sts at beg of next 12 rows, 3 sts at beg of next 10 rows and 4 sts at beg of next 2 rows. 128 sts.
Continue without shaping for 4 rows more.
Next row K to last 5 sts, turn.
Next row P to last 5 sts, turn.
Next row K to last 10 sts, turn.
Continue working 5 sts less on every row 11 times more, then K to end.
P 1 row.
**Continue in st st, working 4 rows B, 4 rows A, 4 rows C, 4 rows A, 4 rows D, 4 rows A, 4 rows E and 9 rows A.
Bind off loosely.

Knitted bikini pants front

Using No.2 needles and A, cast on 20 sts.
Work in st st for 24 rows.
Inc one st at each end of next and every following 4th row 5 times in all, then at each end of every other row 3 times, ending with a P row.
Cast on 2 sts at beg of next 6 rows, 3 sts at beg of next 10 rows, 5 sts at beg of next 2 rows and 20 sts at beg of next 2 rows. 128 sts.
Continue without shaping for 6 rows more.
Continue as given for Back from ** to end.

Knitted bikini top right half

Using No.2 needles and B, cast on 96 sts.
Work in g st for 4 rows.
Attach A and continuing in st st, work stripe patt as on Pants (i.e. 4 rows each of A, C, A, D, A, E, A, B) throughout, *at the same time,* shaping as follows:
1st row K45, K up 1, K1, K up 1, K50.
2nd row P.
3rd row K46, K up 1, K1, K up 1, K51.
4th row Bind off 3 sts, P to end.
5th row Bind off 2 sts, K45, K up 1, K1, K up 1, K to end.
6th row As 4th.
7th row Bind off 2 sts, K44, K up 1, K1, K up 1, K to end.
8th row As 4th.
9th row Bind off 2 sts, K43, K up 1, K1, K up 1, K to end.
10th row As 4th.
11th row Bind off 2 sts, K42, K up 1, K1, K up 1, K to end.
12th row As 4th. 85 sts.
Bind off 2 sts at beg of next 8 rows. 69 sts.
21st row K2 tog, K to end.
22nd row Bind off 2 sts, P to end.
Rep last 2 rows twice more. 60 sts.
Dec one st at each end of next and every other row 12 times, then at each end of every 4th row until 4 sts rem, ending with a P row.
Next row K1, K2 tog, K1. 3 sts. Bind off.

Knitted bikini top left half

Work as given for Right Half, reversing all shaping.

Crochet bikini pants front

Using No.D hook and A, ch18.
1st row 1dc into 3rd ch from hook, *1dc into next ch, rep from * to end. 16 sts.
2nd row Ch3 to count as first dc, 1dc into each dc to end.

3rd row Attach B, ch1, 1sc into each dc to end.
4th row Using A, ch3, 1dc into each sc to end.
5th row As 2nd.
The last 3 rows form patt and are rep throughout.
Work 2 rows more.
Inc one st at each end of next 2 rows, 2 sts at each end of next 9 rows, 3 sts at each end of next 4 rows and 25 sts at each end of next row. 130 sts.
Continue without shaping for 13 rows more, ending with a 3rd patt row. Fasten off.

Crochet bikini pants back

Using No.D hook and A, ch18.
Work in stripe patt as given for Front, inc one st at each end of first 3 rows, 2 sts at each end of next 12 rows, 3 sts at each end of next 6 rows, 4 sts at each end of next row and 8 sts at each end of next row. 130 sts.
Continue without shaping for 13 rows more, ending with a 3rd patt row. Fasten off.

Crochet bikini top right half

Work throughout in 3-row stripe patt as on Pants.
Using No.D hook and A, ch101.
Work first 3 rows as given for Pants Front. 99 sts.
4th row Using A, ss to 8th st, ch3, 1dc into each of next 40 sts, 2dc into next st, 1dc into next st, 2dc into next st, 1dc into each st to last 4 sts, turn. 90 sts.
5th row Using A, ss to 5th st, ch3, 1dc into each of next 40 sts, 2dc into next st, 1dc into next st, 2dc into next st, 1dc into each st to last 7 sts, turn. 81 sts.
6th row Using B, ch1, 1sc into each st to end.
7th row Using A, ss to 5th st, ch3, 1dc into each of next 37 sts, 2dc into next st, 1 dc into next st, 2dc into next st, 1dc into each st to last 6 sts, turn. 73 sts.
8th row Using A, ss to 7th st, ch3, 1dc into each of next 24 sts, 2dc into next st, 1dc

into next st, 2dc into next st, 1dc into each st to last 4 sts, turn. 65 sts.

9th row As 6th.

10th row Using A, ss to 7th st, ch3, 1 dc into each of next 19 sts, 2 dc into next st, 1 dc into next st, 2dc into next st, 1 dc into each st to last 2 sts, turn. 59 sts.

11th row Using A, ss to 3rd st, ch3, 1dc into each of next 32 sts, 2dc into next st, 1dc into next st, 2dc into next st, 1dc into each st to last 2 sts, turn. 57 sts.

12th row As 6th.
Continue in patt, dec 2 sts at each end of next 8 rows in A only (all rows in B are worked without dec throughout). 25 sts.

25th row Dec 2 sts at beg of row and one st at end.

26th row Dec one st at beg of row and 2 sts at end.

28th and 29th rows As 25th and 26th. 13 sts.
Dec one st at each end of next 2 rows in A, then at each end of every other row in A 3 times. 3 sts. Fasten off.

Crochet bikini top left half

Work as given for Right Half, reversing all shaping.

Swimsuit back

Using No.2 straight needles and A, cast on 18 sts.
Work in st st, inc one st at each end of first and 3rd rows.
P1 row.
Continue in st st, casting on 2 sts at beg of next 22 rows, 3 sts at beg of next 14 rows and 4 sts at beg of next 8 rows. 140 sts.
****Continue without shaping for 6½in, ending with a P row.
Next row K1, sl 1, K1, psso, K to last 3 sts, K2 tog, K1.
Work 5 rows more.
Rep last 6 rows once more. 136 sts.
Next row K1, sl 1, K1, psso, K32, K2 tog, K62, sl 1, K1, psso, K32, K2 tog, K1.
Work 5 rows more.
Next row K1, sl 1, K1, psso, K30, K2 tog, K62, sl 1, K1, psso, K32, K2 tog, K1.
Continue dec in this manner

every 6th row 3 times more.
Work 15 rows more. 116 sts.
Next row K27, K up 1, K62, K up 1, K27.
Work 5 rows more.
Next row K28, K up 1, K62, K up 1, K28.
Work 5 rows more.
Next row K1, K up 1, K28, K up 1, K62, K up 1, K28, K up 1, K1.
Continue inc at each side of center 62 sts on every 6th row twice more, *at the same time*, continue inc at each end of every 6th row until there are 140 sts.
Continue without shaping until work measures 19½in from beg, ending with a P row.

Divide for neck

Next row K70, turn and slip rem sts on spare needle.
Bind off 2 sts at beg of each of next 10 rows.
P 1 row.
Dec one st at each end of next and every other row 15 times in all, then at each end of every 4th row twice and then at each end of every 6th row 5 times. 6 sts.
Continue without shaping, if necessary, until strap is long enough to reach shoulder. Bind off.
With RS facing, attach yarn to sts on extra needle and K to end.
Complete to correspond with first side.
Fasten off.

Swimsuit front

Using No.2 needles and A, cast on 18 sts.
Work 8 rows st st.
Continue in st st, inc one st at each end of next and every following 4th row 3 times more, then at each end of every other row twice, ending with a P row.
Cast on 2 sts at beg of next 20 rows, 3 sts at beg of next 4 rows, 6 sts at beg of next 4 rows and 17 sts at beg of next 2 rows. 140 sts.
Continue as given for Back from ** to end.

Finishing

Knitted bikini. Press work

lightly using a cool iron.
Join side and gusset seams of Pants. Using set of 4 No.2 needles and B, with RS facing, pick up and K 160 sts around each leg.
Join. K 4 rounds. Bind off.
Fold last 9 rows at top of Pants to inside and slip-stitch in place. Thread elastic through hem.
Using No.2 straight needles and B, with RS facing, pick up and K 96 sts along inner edge of each Top piece. K 4 rows. Bind off. Pick up and K 106 sts along outer edge of each piece. K 4 rows. Bind off.
Sew two pieces tog at front, overlapping the right half over the left half by 4in.
Make 4 cords each 12in long. Sew one to each side of Back and one to each point of Top (to tie at back of neck).
Press all seams.
Crochet Bikini. Press as given for Knitted Bikini.
Join side and gusset seams of Pants. With RS facing, work one row sc in A then one row sc in B around top edge and around legs. Sew elastic inside waist with herringbone-casing.
Work one row sc in A and one row in B around all edges of Top. Sew the two pieces tog at front, overlapping them by 5in. Make 4 cords each about 14in long, and sew one to top of each front and one to each back corner to tie. Press all seams.
Swimsuit. Press as given for Knitted Bikini.
Join shoulder, side and gusset seams.
Using set of 4 No.2 needles and D, with RS facing, pick up and K 320 sts around neck. Divide sts and join.
Work 4 rounds K1, P1 rib. Bind off in rib.
Using set of 4 No.2 needles and D, with RS facing, pick up and K 160 sts around each armhole and work as given for neck.
Using set of 4 No.2 needles and B, with RS facing, pick up and K 148 sts around each leg. Work 3 rounds in rib. Break off B and attach C. K 1 round, then rib 3 rounds. Rep with D and E. Bind off in rib. Press all seams.

Knit and Crochet Abbreviations

In pattern instructions for both knitting and crochet it is usual for a shortened form to be used for the most common terms. Here we give a list of the abbreviations you are likely to find in Creative Hands.

alt	= alternate
beg	= beginning
ch	= chain
cl	= cluster
cm	= centimeter
dc	= double crochet
dec	= decrease
dtr	= double treble
gr(s)	= group(s)
grm(s)	= gram(s)
hdc	= half double
in	= inch(es)
inc	= increase
K	= knit
K-wise	= knitwise
KB	= knit into back of stitch
M1K	= make 1 knitwise by picking up loop between stitch just worked and following stitch and knit into the back of it
M1P	= make 1 purlwise by picking up loop between stitch just worked and following stitch and purling into the back of it
No.	= number
P	= purl
P-wise	= purlwise
patt	= pattern
PB	= purl into back of stitch
psso	= pass slip stitch over
rem	= remaining
rep	= repeat
RS	= right side
sc	= single crochet
sl 1	= slip 1 knitwise
sl 1P	= slip 1 purlwise
sp(s)	= space(s)
sl st	= slip stitch in knitting
ss	= slip stitch in crochet
st(s)	= stitch(es)
st st	= stocking stitch
tbl	= through back of loop(s)
tog	= together
tr	= treble crochet
TW2	= twist 2 by knitting into front of 2nd stitch then front of first stitch on left-hand needle and slipping 2 stitches off needle together
TW2B	= twist 2 back by knitting into back of 2nd stitch then back of first stitch on left-hand needle and slipping 2 stitches off needle together
WS	= wrong side
ytb	= yarn to back
ytf	= yarn to front
yoh	= yarn over hook
yon	= yarn over needle

Baby's jacket

This beautiful baby's jacket is worked in a single piece, so that only the sleeves have to be joined. Crocheted in a pretty shell pattern, the jacket has a bobble edging and a frill around the yoke. The neck ties with a drawstring, which is threaded through the top of the jacket.

Size

Directions are for 18in chest
Length, 9½in
Sleeve seam, 5in

Gauge
5 clusters and 12 rows to 4in over patt worked on No.D hook

Materials

Columbia Minerva Baby Nantuk 4 ounces
One No. D (3.00 mm) crochet hook
Small amount of white angora (optional)

Main section

Beg at neck and with No.D hook, ch91.

1st row (RS) 1dc into 3rd ch from hook, 1dc into each of the next 12ch, 3dc into next ch, 1dc into each of next 14ch, 3dc into next ch, 1dc into each of next 29ch, (3dc into next ch, 1dc into each of next 14ch) twice. 97 sts.

2nd row Ch1, *1sc into front loop only of next dc, rep from * to end.

3rd row Ch3, working into both loops of each st, 1dc into each of next 14sc, 5dc into next sc, 1dc into each of next 16sc, 5dc into next sc,

1dc into each of next 31sc, 5dc into next sc, 1dc into each of next 16sc, 5dc into next sc, 1dc into each sc to end. 113dc.

4th row As 2nd.

5th row Ch3, 1dc into each of next 16sc, 5dc into next sc, 1dc into each of next 20sc, 5dc into next sc, 1dc into each of next 35sc, 5dc into next sc, 1dc into each of next 20sc, 5dc into next sc, 1dc into each sc to end. 129dc.
Continue inc in this manner every other row twice more, ending with an inc row. 161dc.

10th row (WS) Ch1, skip 1dc, (yrh, insert hook into back loop of next dc, yrh and draw up a loop to ¼in, yrh and draw through 2 loops, yrh and draw through rem 2 loops – called a long dc –) 5 times into next dc, *skip 1dc, 1sc into both loops of next dc, 5 long dc – called 1cl – into back loop of next dc, rep from * to last 2 sts, skip 1dc, 1sc into 3rd of ch3. 40cl.

11th row Ch3, 1 long dc into first sc (edge st), *1sc into 3rd of 5 long dc, 1cl into back loop of next sc, rep from * to end, finishing with 1sc into 3rd of 5 long dc, 2

long dc into turning ch.

12th row Ch1, (1cl into back loop of next sc, 1sc into 3rd of 5 long dc) 6 times, skip 7cl, 1sc into 3rd long dc of next cl, (1cl into back loop of next sc, 1sc into 3rd of 5 long dc) 12 times, skip 7cl, 1sc into 3rd long dc of next cl, (1cl into back loop of next sc, 1sc into 3rd of 5 long dc) 5 times, 1cl into back loop of next sc, 1sc into 3rd of ch3. 24cl.

13th row As 11th but working the 6th and 18th cl between the 2sc at underarms.

14th row Ch1, *1cl into back loop of next sc, 1sc into 3rd of 5 long dc, rep from * to end working last sc into 3rd of ch3.

15th row As 11th.
Rep last 2 rows 7 times more, then 14th row once more. Fasten off.

Sleeves

With WS facing, attach yarn to same dc as 6th sc of 12th row, ch1, (1cl into back loop of next sc, 1sc into 3rd of 5 long dc) 8 times working the last sc into same dc as first sc of back, turn.
Continue on these 8cl for 14

Stitch detail showing body, yoke and frill

rows more.

Next row Ch 1, *1sc into each of next 2 long dc, skip 1 long dc, 1sc into each of next 2 long dc, skip 1sc, rep from * 7 times more, 1sc into turning ch. 34sc.
Work 5 rows sc.
Fasten off.
Work a second sleeve in the same manner.

Edging

With RS facing, attach yarn to lower corner of right front, *ch2, (yrh, insert hook into edge st of 2nd row, yrh and draw up a loop to ¼in) 4 times, yrh and draw through all 9 loops on hook – called a bobble –, rep from * up right front edge to neck working a bobble into every other row (i.e. rows with 2 long dc at each end), 1sc into each st around neck edge, then work down left front edge to correspond with first side, turn.

Next row *Ch2, 1 bobble into ch2 sp of previous row, rep from * up front edge, 1sc into first sc at neck, ** skip 1sc, 5dc into next sc, skip 1sc, 1sc into next sc, rep from ** around neck, then work down right front edge to correspond with first side.
Fasten off.

Yoke frill

With RS facing, attach yarn to left front at beg of 2nd sc row from neck, ch1, 1sc into each st of this row to end, turn.

Next row Ch4, 2tr into first sc (edge st), 3tr into each sc to end.
Fasten off.
Attach angora if desired and work ss into each tr to end.
Fasten off.

Finishing

Press work lightly under a damp cloth, using a warm iron.
Join sleeve seams.
Using 4 strands of yarn, make a twisted cord and thread at neck edge.
Press seams.

2225

This appealing caterpillar is designed as an unusual toy or mascot for children of all ages, but it can also double as a sturdy playroom seat. The materials used for making the caterpillar are cheap and easy to buy, and it is made in such a way that it will stand up well to the wear and tear of play.

To make the caterpillar

You will need:

- [ ] 1 yard pink felt
- [ ] $\frac{1}{4}$ yard purple felt
- [ ] $1\frac{1}{4}$ yards lime green fabric, 36 inches wide
- [ ] 3 yards emerald green fabric, 36 inches wide
- [ ] 3 lengths of 1 inch thick foam rubber, each 6 feet long by 18 inches wide (these lengths may be made up from shorter lengths)
- [ ] 2 18-inch squares 1 inch thick foam rubber
- [ ] 2 bags foam rubber chips
- [ ] 1 18-inch diameter foam rubber pillow form (or cut a circle from 3 inch thick foam)
- [ ] 2 30-inch cardboard mailing tubes, inside diameter 2 inches
- [ ] Rubber cement
- [ ] newspaper
- [ ] string
- [ ] thick cardboard
- [ ] 5 inch length of dowel
- [ ] toymaker's needle or carpet needle
- [ ] 2 skeins 6-strand embroidery floss, emerald green

To prepare the stuffing

Cut each 6 foot length of foam in half lengthwise. Cut the mailing tubes into 9 inch lengths. Smear rubber cement down one side of a piece of tube and place it over the short end of one foam length. Roll the rubber, without compressing it, around the tube. The circumference of the roll when fully wound should be about 29 inches and the diameter about $9\frac{1}{2}$ inches.

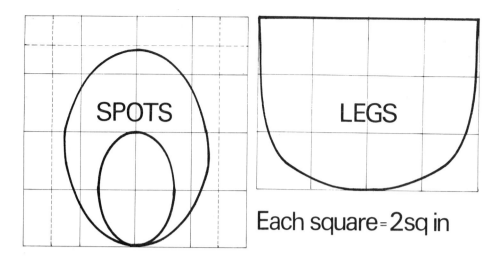

SPOTS

LEGS

Each square = 2 sq in

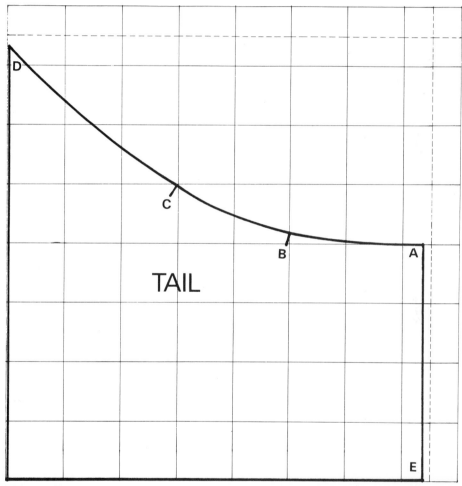

TAIL

Tie a length of string around the middle of the roll. Grip the roll firmly between your knees, compressing it as much as possible, and tie a string around each end, about $\frac{1}{2}$ inch from the edge (Fig. 1). Smear each end of the inside of the mailing tube with rubber cement, and stuff it loosely with crumpled newspaper. Treat all the rolls except one in the same way. The exception will form the neck and should not be stuffed with newspaper. To attach the pillow which forms the head to the neck, cut a piece of cardboard 3 inches square and a length of string about 24 inches long. Thread one end of the string into the toymaker's or carpet needle and push it through the circular pillow about 6 inches from the edge, then push it through the cardboard square. Take the needle back through the cardboard about $1\frac{1}{2}$ inches away from the first hole and push it back through the pillow. Pull the ends of the string even and push them through the mailing tube without the newspaper stuffing. Cut nicks across the center of the length of dowel and knot the ends of string around it, pulling them up as tightly as possible (Fig. 2). Cut a piece of foam and stick it over the depression made in the front of the pillow. Cut a 15 inch diameter circle of 1 inch thick foam and stick it to the front of the pillow.

To make the body

Draw up the pattern pieces for the tail, legs and spots from the graph pattern given here in which 1 square equals 2 inches. $\frac{1}{2}$ inch seam allowance is given throughout, unless otherwise stated. Cut two tail pieces, remembering to reverse the pattern piece if necessary, and 12 legs in emerald green fabric; 12 legs in pink felt; 12 larger spots in pink felt and 12 smaller spots in purple felt.

To make the legs, place a green leg piece to a pink leg piece, right sides together, and stitch. Leave the straight edge open. Turn to the right side and stuff loosely with foam chips. Overcast the raw edges together and repeat for the remaining 11 legs.

For the underbody, cut two pieces from the lime green fabric each measuring 16 inches by 38 inches. Join two short edges. For the top body, cut two pieces from the emerald green fabric, one 16 inches by 38 inches and one 16 inches by 24 inches. Join two short edges. With right sides together, join the two tail pieces along the curved edges A–B and C–D. B–C is left open for stuffing. Open the tail out flat and join the straight edge E–A–E to the short edge of the shorter upper body piece.

To make the segments, measure 4 inches

away from the tail join along the top body. Mark this point at both edges of the fabric with a large basting stitch. Make another two basting stitches 8 inches away from the first pair. Make 8 more sets of marker stitches at intervals of 4 inches and 8 inches alternately (Fig. 3). Baste and stitch a pair of pink spots on each 8 inch segment, positioning the spots at a slant. Stitch the smaller purple spots on top of the pink ones. The last pair of spots is positioned on the tail 1 inch away from the tail join.

With the green side of each leg facing the right side of every 8 inch segment, baste the straight edges to the sides of

each segment. The last pair of legs is basted to the tail under the spots. Place the right side of the underbody to the right side of the top body, with the legs sandwiched in between. Match the underbody seam to the top body seam. Baste and stitch the long straight edges together.

Fold the top body along the upper join of the tail and baste the edges together from the tail tip D to the point where the top body joins the underbody. Continue basting the edges of the underbody together, but increase the seam allowance so that at the lower edge it measures $1\frac{1}{2}$ inches (Fig. 4). Machine stitch, trim away the excess seam allowance and

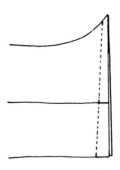

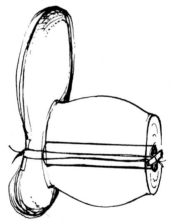

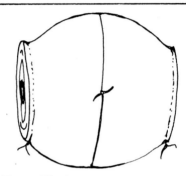

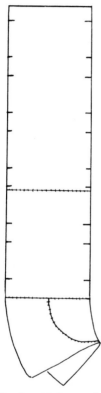

Fig. 1. The foam roll tied with string at the center and at each edge

Fig. 2. The head stuffing secured to the neck segment with string and a length of dowel

Fig. 3. Basting stitches mark the position of the segment divisions along the body

Fig. 4. Fold the tail and take a tapering seam allowance along the open edge

Fig. 5. The position of the features on the face

turn the body to the right side.

To gather each segment, thread a sewing needle with 36 inches of 6-strand floss used double. Starting at the center of the top body on the tail join, make large, even running stitches along the join, across the underbody and back over the top body to the starting point. A chalk line may be drawn across the underbody for guidance. Sew around every segment in the same way. There will be 11 gathering lines in all.

To stuff the body

Push one of the foam rubber rolls down to the tail. Position the end of the roll under the first row of gathering, and pull up the threads firmly around it.

The easiest way to do this is to place the toy on the floor and press down with one foot on the foam to compress it. Grip the gathering threads and pull up. Tie in a firm knot and darn in the end to secure. Run a gathering thread around the end seam on the underbody section of the tail and draw up as tightly as possible. Stuff the tail through the opening B–C and overcast to close.

Put six handfuls of foam rubber chips on top of the foam rubber roll to pad the next segment slightly without

reducing the toy's flexibility, then push the next roll into place. Draw up the gathering threads in the same way to enclose the ends. Continue to stuff along the body in the same way, alternating loose stuffing with foam rolls. Put the neck roll into the last segment and push the excess body fabric between the neck and the head.

The head

The face. Cut a 16 inch diameter circle of emerald green fabric. For the eyes, cut two cardboard ovals each 5 inches long by $3\frac{1}{2}$ inches across the widest part. Glue a layer of 1 inch thick foam rubber on one side. Cut two ovals of lime green fabric each about $1\frac{1}{2}$ inches larger all around than the cardboard ovals. Run a gathering thread around the outer edge. Place the wrong side to the foam padding on the cardboard and draw up the gathering thread. Stick the excess material to the wrong side of the cardboard. Cut two ovals of pink felt 4 inches long by $2\frac{1}{2}$ inches across the widest part and sew them to the centers of the lime green eyes. Cut two purple ovals 2 inches long by $1\frac{1}{2}$ inches wide and sew them to the lower part of the pink ovals.

For the nose, cut a purple felt oval the

same size as the cardboard ovals used for the eyes. Cut a piece of 1 inch thick foam to the same size as the pink ovals used for the eyes. Run a gathering thread around the edge of the purple felt oval and draw it up to enclose and compress the nose foam.

For the mouth, cut a length of 1 inch thick foam 8 inches long by $\frac{1}{2}$ inch wide. Cut a piece of pink felt 2 inches by $8\frac{1}{2}$ inches. Overcast the long edges together around the foam and gather the short edges. Run a gathering thread along one long edge of the felt and draw it up to curve the strip into a smiling mouth. Cut a piece of pink felt $\frac{1}{2}$ inch wide by $2\frac{1}{2}$ inches long for the upper lip. To assemble the face (Fig. 5) find the center of the emerald green circle. Then stick the nose with the top of the oval just below the center. Stick the eyes, just touching each other, above the nose. The upper lip is overlapped by the nose for $\frac{1}{2}$ inch and the mouth is placed to overlap the lower end of the upper lip by $\frac{1}{2}$ inch, so that the upper lip measures $1\frac{1}{2}$ inches. Sew all the features in place from the back of the fabric.

To join the head to the body

For the back of the head, join pieces of emerald green fabric to give a strip 50 inches long by 10 inches wide. Fold it in half with the short edges together and cut along one edge of the material so that the width tapers evenly from 10 inches in the center to 6 inches on each side. Join the short edge with right sides together. Stitch the face to the long straight edge. Run a gathering thread around the tapered edge. Pull the head over the pillow and foam circle from the front and draw up the gathering thread as tightly as possible. Using the toymaker's or carpet needle and embroidery floss, sew the head firmly to the neck.

Antennae

Cut two lengths of 1 inch thick foam each 8 inches by 11 inches. Roll each up lengthwise, and bind with thread to secure. Cut two pieces of emerald green fabric 9 inches by 11 inches. Turn in one long raw edge for $\frac{3}{4}$ inch and sew the fabric strip around the foam, overlapping the long edges rather more at one end to give a tapered shape.

For the knobs at the ends of the antennae, cut two circles of lime green fabric each 5 inches in diameter. Run a gathering thread around the outer edges.

Stuff the circle with loose foam and draw up the gathering threads. Sew one knob to the tapered end of each antenna. Stitch the antennae firmly in position to the top of the head.

Bright flowers for summer

The bold, bright flowers worked across the bodice of this sundress make it especially pretty and gay. The simple daisy shapes used are worked in two basic stitches, using cotton floss.

Materials required:
- ☐ D.M.C. 6-Strand Floss in the following colors: 817 cardinal red, 921 orange, 783 amber gold, white, 471 light moss green, 3345 moss green
- ☐ J. & P. coats embroidery/crewel needle, No.5
- ☐ dressmakers' carbon paper, wheel or
- • tracing paper for transferring design

Working the embroidery
Before making the sundress, transfer the design for the embroidery to the bodice fabric, positioning it as indicated. There are two methods which are suitable for transferring the design: either baste the outline through tracing or tissue paper, then tear the paper away, or use a wheel and dressmakers' carbon paper.

Use the tracing pattern for positioning the colors, and work with six strands of floss in the needle. The stems are worked in stem stitch and the remaining areas of the design are worked in satin stitch, with interlocking groups of stitches on the larger leaf surfaces. The center of each flower is worked in white, with a white strip extending into each petal.

Adapting the motif
Because the floral design is simple and straightforward, it is suitable for casual clothes and children's garments as well as for household linens. The number of flowers can easily be reduced, if required, to fit the area on which the embroidery is to be worked. A simple child's smock would be summery and appealing worked in bright colors, perhaps on a striped fabric. The embroidery might also be centered on the back of a beach wrap or caftan, in a combination of washable threads.

Tracing pattern for the floral embroidery. The colors indicated on the design are in D.M.C. 6-Strand Floss

817 cardinal red
921 orange
783 amber gold
471 light moss green
3345 moss green
white (flower and petal centers)

stem stitch

satin stitch

CRAFTS

Jewelry from clay

These attractive and original necklaces are made from oven-baked clay beads, painted with bright enamel and threaded or linked with jeweler's wire. The beads can be left plain, interspersed with bought beads for contrast, or made in a variety of shapes and sizes to create individual and unusual jewelry.

You will need:
- [ ] oven bake clay, such as Ceraclay
- [ ] enamel
- [ ] round wooden toothpicks
- [ ] silver, copper or anodized aluminum wire
- [ ] jewelry saw frame and blades
- [ ] two pairs of flat pliers, one pair of round pliers
- [ ] hand drill
- [ ] No.4 and No.6 knitting needles

To make the beads

Mix the clay, following the instructions given on the package. Mix only small amounts of clay at a time, as large quantities left standing tend to harden. Pinch off enough clay to make a bead of the required size, and roll it in the palm of the hand until it is smooth and round. To make a hole through the bead without spoiling the shape, let the bead lie in the palm of the hand and press the point of a toothpick through the bead until the point touches the palm. Turn the bead over and repeat from the other side.

The red choker

Make 26 clay beads, grading the sizes from a large bead to place at the center front through successively smaller pairs, so that the beads at the center back of the choker are approximately half the size of the front ones. Leave the beads to dry overnight.

Bake the beads in the oven to harden them finally, following the instructions on the package.

When the beads are cool, they are ready to paint. A useful paint rack can be made by rolling out a long sausage of clay and sticking a row of toothpicks vertically into it. First paint the top half of the bead, then turn it upside down, place it on the paint rack and paint the underside. The beads illustrated here are painted with bright red enamel.

Measure the circumference of the neck and cut off a length of 16 gauge wire equal to this length. Bend the wire gently so that it curves around the neck. Using the round pliers, bend one end of the wire over to form a ring (Fig. 1a). Lay the painted beads out in the size sequence and begin threading them onto the wire. The necklace illustrated here has small black glass beads placed between the red beads, and the necklace is finished off at each end with two black beads. Use the round pliers to bend the other end of the wire over to form a loop (Fig. 1b).

The links

Take a hand drill and clamp it in a bench vice in such a way that the drill may be freely rotated. Take the No.4 knitting needle and place the pointed end in the drill (Fig. 2).

Take a length of 18 gauge wire and make a right-angled bend at one end. Hook this short end into any one of the spaces

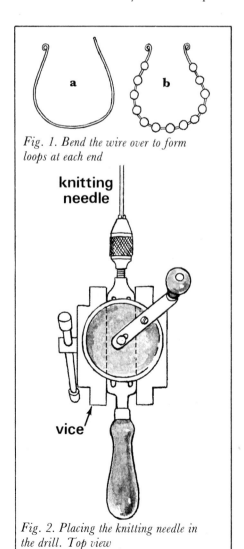

Fig. 1. Bend the wire over to form loops at each end

knitting needle

vice

Fig. 2. Placing the knitting needle in the drill. Top view

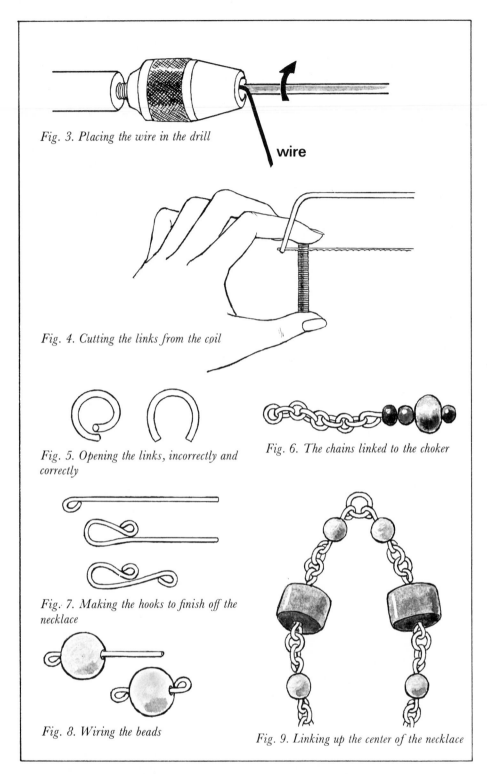

Fig. 3. Placing the wire in the drill

wire

Fig. 4. Cutting the links from the coil

Fig. 5. Opening the links, incorrectly and correctly

Fig. 6. The chains linked to the choker

Fig. 7. Making the hooks to finish off the necklace

Fig. 8. Wiring the beads

Fig. 9. Linking up the center of the necklace

securely. Always use two pairs of flat pliers to open the links (Fig. 5) and to pinch them closed.

Make two chains each composed of eight links. Link the chains to the ends of the choker as shown (Fig. 6).

Make two hooks (Fig. 7) and link to the chains to complete the necklace.

Green and white beads

Make 11 pairs of green beads, graded in size, by rolling out a "sausage" of clay, thicker at one end and tapering toward the other end. Slice off the beads with a sharp knife and make the central holes with a toothpick. Make 23 small round beads as described above, and bake the beads in the same way. Paint the large tubular beads bright green with enamel. The smaller beads are left plain. Wire each bead as follows: pass one end of a length of wire through the bead, and use the round pliers to bend the end over to form a loop (Fig. 8). Cut the wire, leaving a length sufficient to make a loop on the other side of the bead.

Make a number of links as described for the red choker, and pass a link through the loop at each side of each bead. Begin the necklace at the center front with a small white bead, and use a third link at each side to join each side of the center bead to the largest of the pairs of green beads. Continue linking the beads in this way until ten green beads and eleven white beads are linked, ending with a white bead at each end. Join the two white beads with a slightly larger link, made on a No.6 knitting needle (Fig. 9). Link two more white beads into this larger link, and continue threading the beads until there are 12 white and 12 green beads in the upper part of the necklace, ending with a green bead at each end. From the last bead link two small links and one large link. Make a hook as described above to complete the necklace.

Ways with beads

Beads can be made in any shape or size, from huge round or square beads to wear as eye-catching pendants to tiny beads for a delicate necklace. As well as painting or varnishing, decorative effects can be achieved by making impressions in the surface of the clay while it is still soft or sticking small objects such as shells into the clay.

Jeweler's findings such as bases for rings and cufflinks can be bought at most craft shops.

between the jaws of the chuck (Fig. 3). The length of wire should pass over the front of the knitting needle.

Now grip the knitting needle with the right hand as if it were a pencil, placing the thumb on the section of wire which passes over the knitting needle. With the left hand, slowly turn the handle of the drill so that the knitting needle revolves in the direction indicated in Fig. 3. This will make the wire wind up on the needle to form a coil. Guide the wire with the thumb as it is winding so that the coil is very tight. When the wire is all wound around the needle, the coil

can be pulled off.

To cut links from the coil, take the coil in the left hand and hold it vertically between the thumb and first finger, with the coil nearest the body. Still holding the coil between the thumb and first finger, press the coil against a table top. Use the jewelry saw to cut through the top of the coil (Fig. 4).

As the blade cuts through the top of the coil, the first link falls away. Always hold the coil tightly between the thumb and first finger while sawing. Do not use too thick a blade to cut the links or the gap in the link will be too large to close

QUICK MAKE
Gaucho pants

These attractive gaucho pants are quick and simple to make. They can be cut to the knee in a tweed fabric as shown here, or the pattern can be extended to full length, and made up in a more exotic fabric such as silk or satin for evening wear.

Fabrics and notions

You will need:

- [ ] 1½ yards 54 inch wide fabric, all sizes, or
- [ ] 2⅜ yards 36 inch wide fabric, all sizes
- [ ] ⅛ yard 36 inch wide interfacing
- [ ] sewing thread to match fabric
- [ ] 8 inch skirt zipper
- [ ] ½ inch button or two hooks and bars
- [ ] graph paper for pattern

The pattern

The pattern given here is for sizes 10, 12, 14 and 16.

Using the graph paper, draw up each pattern piece to scale. A seam allowance of ⅝ inch is included on all edges and a hem allowance of 3 inches is given.

To make the pants

1. With right sides together, baste and stitch the front darts. Press the darts toward the center front.

2. With right sides together, baste and stitch the back darts. Press the darts toward the center back.

3. With right sides together, matching notches, baste and stitch the backs to the fronts at the side and inner leg edges. Press all seams open.

4. With right sides together, matching notches, baste and stitch the front and back sections together along the center back and center front in one continuous seam, leaving the seam open at the front above the large circle. Press the seam open.

5. Baste the seam allowance on the front opening to the wrong side of the garment and insert the zipper following the instructions given on the zipper package.

6. Baste the interfacing to the wrong side and notched edge of the waistband and catch stitch along the fold line.

7. With right sides together, pin, baste and stitch the interfaced edge of the waistband to the skirt. Turn under the seam allowance on the unstitched edge of the band, baste and press.

8. With right sides together, fold the waistband on the fold line and stitch the ends, stitching the right front edge to the circle. Clip to the circle. Cut away the interfacing close to the stitching and grade seams, cutting across corners.

9. Turn the band to the inside. Baste around all edges. Press. Hem stitch the waistband edge to the machine stitching.

10. Make a hand or machine made button hole in the waistband and sew on the button to close. Or, sew on hooks and bars to close.

11. Try on the gaucho pants and mark the hem line. Turn up the hem on the marked line and baste around the fold edge from the right side of the garment. Press the fold edge only. Trim the hem to an even depth all around. Overcast the raw edge by hand or machine.

12. Sew the hem with invisible hem stitching.

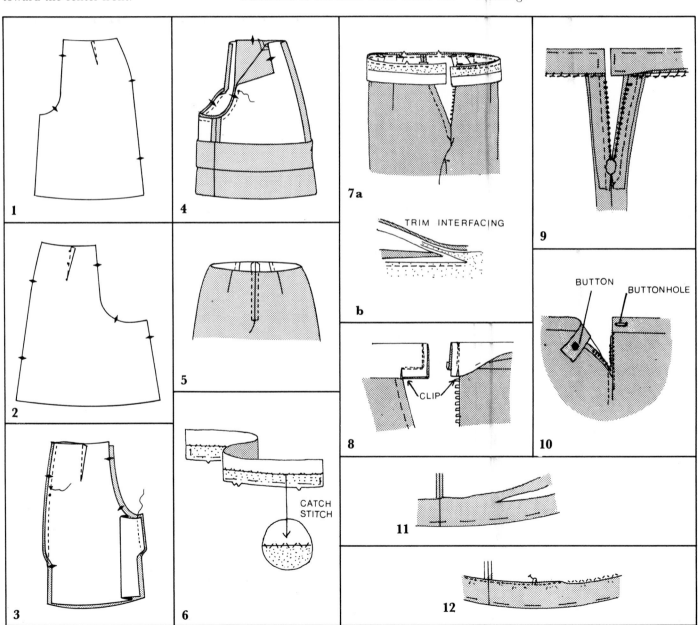

TRIM INTERFACING

CATCH STITCH

CLIP

BUTTON   BUTTONHOLE

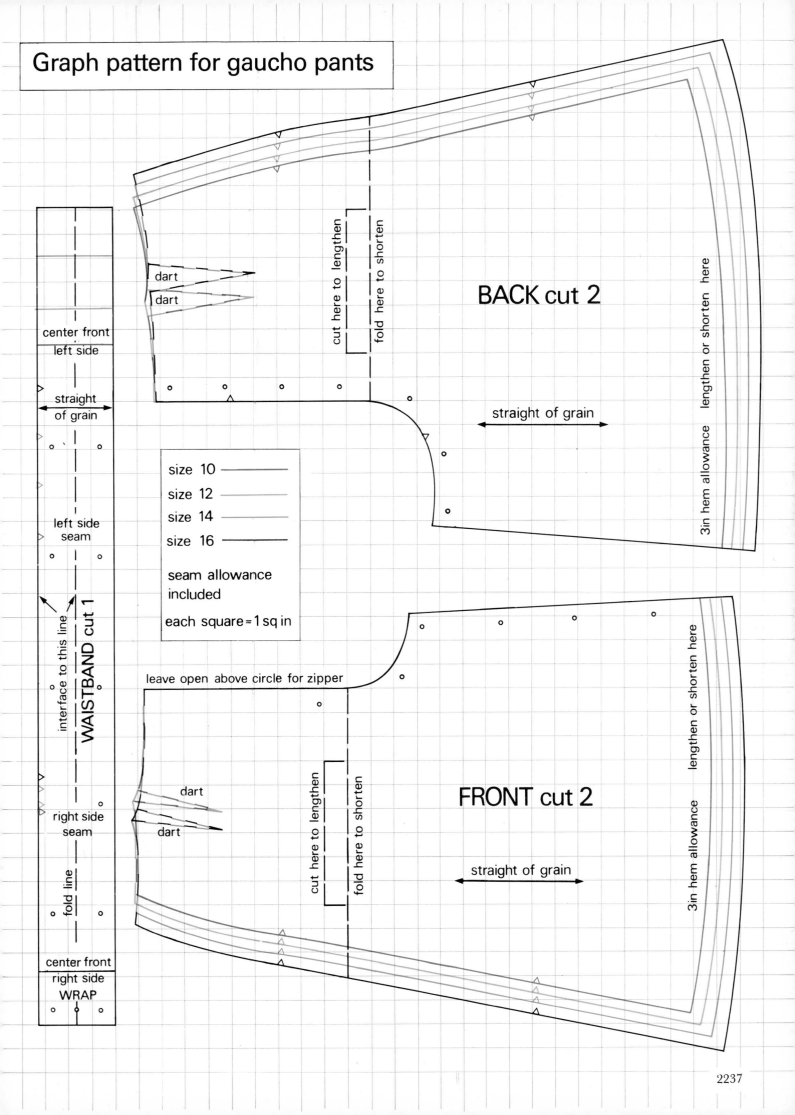

Graph pattern for gaucho pants

BACK cut 2

dart
dart

cut here to lengthen
fold here to shorten

center front
left side

straight
of grain

left side
seam

straight of grain

lengthen or shorten here

3in hem allowance

size 10
size 12
size 14
size 16

seam allowance
included

each square = 1 sq in

interface to this line

WAISTBAND cut 1

right side
seam

fold line

leave open above circle for zipper

FRONT cut 2

dart
dart

cut here to lengthen
fold here to shorten

straight of grain

lengthen or shorten here

3in hem allowance

center front
right side
WRAP

2237

2238

Crochet in chevron

This crocheted bedspread is worked in chevron stripes using three toning shades of rug yarn for a sophisticated effect.

The simple basis of the pattern could, however, be worked to create a rainbow colored bedspread using small amounts of different colors.

Size

About 90in by 63in, adjustable

Gauge

16 sts to 7in and 4 rows to 3in over patt worked on a Jumbo crochet hook

Materials

Aunt Lydia's Rug Yarn 70-yard skeins
12 skeins in each of A, B and C
One Jumbo crochet hook

Bedspread

Using Jumbo hook and A, ch144.

1st row 1sc into 2nd ch from hook, *1sc into next ch, rep from * to end. 143 sts.

2nd row Ch2, 1sc into first sc (edge st), then working into the back loop only of every sc throughout, 1sc into each of next 5sc, *(insert hook into next st and draw through loop) 3 times, yrh and draw through all 4 loops on hook – called 3sc tog – 1sc into each of next 6sc, 3sc into next sc, 1sc into each of next 6sc, rep from * 7 times more, 3sc tog, 1sc into each of next 5sc, 2sc into turning ch.

Rep 2nd row throughout, always working into the back loop only of each sc. Work (4 rows A, 4 rows B, 4 rows C) 10 times or until length desired.
Fasten off.
Press lightly.

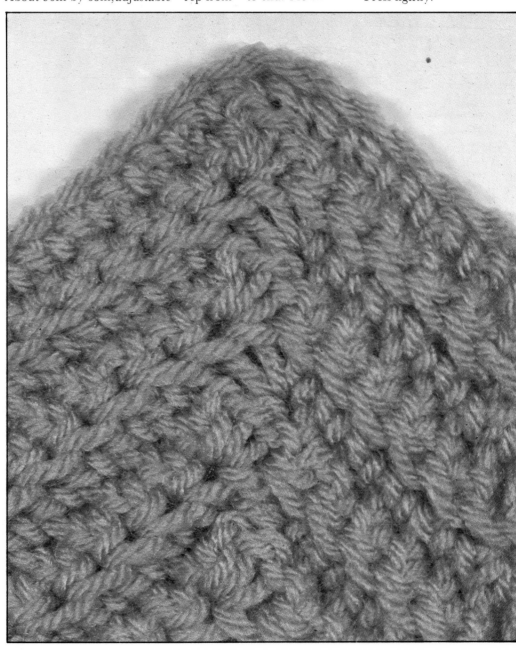

Knit and Crochet Abbreviations

In pattern instructions for both knitting and crochet it is usual for a shortened form to be used for the most common terms. Here we give a list of the abbreviations you are likely to find in Creative Hands.

alt	=	alternate
beg	=	beginning
ch	=	chain
cl	=	cluster
cm	=	centimeter
dc	=	double crochet
dec	=	decrease
dtr	=	double treble
gr(s)	=	group(s)
grm(s)	=	gram(s)
hdc	=	half double
in	=	inch(es)
inc	=	increase
K	=	knit
K-wise	=	knitwise
KB	=	knit into back of stitch
M1K	=	make 1 knitwise by picking up loop between stitch just worked and following stitch and knit into the back of it
M1P	=	make 1 purlwise by picking up loop between stitch just worked and following stitch and purling into the back of it
No.	=	number
P	=	purl
P-wise	=	purlwise
patt	=	pattern
PB	=	purl into back of stitch
psso	=	pass slip stitch over
rem	=	remaining
rep	=	repeat
RS	=	right side
sc	=	single crochet
sl 1	=	slip 1 knitwise
sl 1P	=	slip 1 purlwise
sp(s)	=	space(s)
sl st	=	slip stitch in knitting
ss	=	slip stitch in crochet
st(s)	=	stitch(es)
st st	=	stocking stitch
tbl	=	through back of loop(s)
tog	=	together
tr	=	treble crochet
TW2	=	twist 2 by knitting into front of 2nd stitch then front of first stitch on left-hand needle and slipping 2 stitches off needle together
TW2B	=	twist 2 back by knitting into back of 2nd stitch then back of first stitch on left-hand needle and slipping 2 stitches off needle together
WS	=	wrong side
ytb	=	yarn to back
ytf	=	yarn to front
yoh	=	yarn over hook
yon	=	yarn over needle

KNITTING FOR WOMEN

Couple in cable

Mix and match bright colors to make this eye-catching twinset. The fine stripe in the pullover echoes the color of the cardigan, and the buttons on the cardigan blend with the pullover. The cable motif is repeated on both garments.

Sizes

Directions are for 32in bust
The figures in brackets [ ]
refer to the 34 and 36in bust
Pullover. Length to
shoulder, 20½[21:21½]in
Cardigan. Length to
shoulder, 29½[30:30½]in
Sleeve seam with cuff turned
up, 17[17:17]in

> **Gauge**
> 8 sts and 10 rows to 1in
> over st st worked on No.
> 3 needles

Materials

3-Ply Fingering Yarn
1 oz. skeins
Pullover. 6 [6:7] skeins A
1 [1:1] skein B
Cardigan. 11 [11:12]
skeins B
No. 2 knitting needles
(or Canadian No. 11)
No. 3 knitting needles
(or Canadian No. 10)
One cable needle
Pullover only. One set of 4
No. 2 double-pointed needles
Cardigan only. 9 buttons

Cardigan back

Using No.2 needles and B,
cast on 154[162:170] sts.
Work 9 rows st st, beg with
a K row.
Next row (hem foldline) K.
Change to No.3 needles.
Work 12 rows st st, beg with
a K row.
Next row K3, K2 tog, K to
last 5 sts, K2 tog, K3.
Work 11 rows even.
Rep last 12 rows 11 times
more, then work dec row
once more. 128[136:144] sts.
Continue without shaping
until work measures 22in
from foldline, ending with
a P row.

Shape armholes

Bind off 4 sts at beg of each
of next 2 rows.
Dec one st at each end of
every other row 10[12:14]
times. 100[104:108] sts.
Continue without shaping
until armhole measures
7½[8:8½]in, ending with a
P row.

Shape shoulders

Bind off 9 sts at beg of each
of next 4 rows.
Bind off 9[10:11] sts at beg

of each of next 2 rows.
Bind off rem 46[48:50] sts.

Pocket lining

Using No.3 needles, cast on
40 sts.
Work 50 rows st st, beg with
a K row.
Slip sts on holder.
Make a second lining in the
same manner.

Cardigan left front

Using No.2 needles, cast on
77[81:85] sts.
Work 9 rows st st, beg with
a K row.
Next row (hem foldline) K.
Change to No.3 needles.
1st patt row K27[29:31],
P2, K8, P2, K10[11:12], P2,
K8, P2, K16[17:18].
2nd patt row P16[17:18],
K2, P8, K2, P10[11:12], K2,
P8, K2, P to end.
Rep 1st and 2nd rows twice
more.
7th patt row K27 [29:31],
P2, cable 8 (see Pullover) P2,
K10 [11:12], P2, cable 8,
P2, K16 [17:18].
8th patt row As 2nd.
Rep 1st and 2nd rows twice
more.
These 12 rows form cable patt.
Next row K3, K2 tog tbl,
patt to end.
Patt 11 rows more.
Rep last 12 rows 5 times
more, then work dec row
once more. 70[74:78] sts.
Patt 9 rows more.
Next row (pocket row) Patt
17[19:22], slip next 40 sts
onto holder and leave at
front of work, work across
40 sts of pocket lining, patt
to end of row.
Work 1 row.
Dec at side edge as before
on next and following 12th
rows 6 times in all. 64[68:72]
sts.
Continue without shaping
until work measures the same
as Back to armhole, ending
with a WS row.

Shape armhole

Next row Bind off 4 sts, patt
to end.
Work 1 row.
Dec one st at armhole edge
every other row
10[12:14] times. 50[52:54] sts.
Continue without shaping

until armhole measures
5[5½:6]in, ending at front
edge.

Shape neck

Next row Bind off 13[14:15]
sts, patt to end.
Continue on these 37[38:39]
sts.
Dec one st at neck edge on
each of next 10 rows.
27[28:29] sts.
Continue without shaping
until armhole measures same
as Back, ending at armhole
edge.

Shape shoulder

At arm edge, bind off 9 sts
every other row twice.
Work 1 row.
Bind off rem 9[10:11] sts.

Cardigan right front

Work as given for Left
Front to hem foldline.
Change to No.3 needles.
1st patt row K16[17:18],
P2, K8, P2, K10[11:12], P2,
K8, P2, K to end.
2nd row P27[29:31], K2,
P8, K2, P10[11:12], K2, P8,
K2, P16[17:18].
Rep 1st and 2nd rows twice
more.
7th patt row K16[17:18],
P2, cable 8, P2, K10[11:12],
P2, cable 8, P2, K to end.
8th patt row As 2nd.
Rep 1st and 2nd rows twice
more.
These 12 rows form the cable
patt.
Next row Patt to last 5 sts,
K2 tog, K3.
Patt 11 rows more.
Rep last 12 rows 5 times
more, then work dec row
once more. 70[74:78] sts.
Patt 9 rows.
Next row (pocket row) Patt
13[15:16], slip next 40 sts
onto holder and leave at
front of work, work across
40 sts of second pocket
lining, patt to end of row.
Continue as for Left Front,
reversing all shaping.

Sleeves

Using No.2 needles, cast on
68[72:76] sts.
Work 90 rows K2, P2 rib.
Change to No.3 needles.

1st patt row K28[30:32],
P2, K8, P2, K to end.
2nd patt row P28[30:32],
K2, P8, K2, P to end.
These 2 rows set the position
of cable patt.
Continue as established,
working cable as before, inc
one st at each end of next and
every following 10th row
until there are 96[100:104]sts.
Continue without shaping
until sleeve seam measures
23in from beg, ending with a
WS row.

Shape cap

Keeping cable patt correct,
bind off 4 sts at beg of each
of next 2 rows.
Dec one st at each end of
every other row 20[22:24]
times. 48 sts.
Next row (WS) *P2 tog, rep
from * to end.
Bind off, working 2 sts tog
all along the row.

Collar

Using No.2 needles, cast on
146[150:154] sts.
Work 8 rows K2, P2 rib, beg
RS rows with K2 and WS
rows with P2.
Next row K2, P2 tog tbl,
rib to last 4 sts, P2 tog, K2.
Rib 7 rows.
Rep last 8 rows 7 times more.
Bind off in rib.

Button band

Using No.2 needles, cast on
12 sts.
Work 236[242:248] rows K1,
P1 rib.
Bind off in rib.

Buttonhole band

Using No.2 needles, cast
on 12 sts.
Work 10[14:18] rows K1, P1
rib.
1st buttonhole row Rib 4,
bind off 4 sts, rib to end.
2nd buttonhole row Rib 4,
cast on 4 sts over those bound-
off on previous row, rib to
end.
Rib 26 rows.
Rep last 28 rows 7 times
more, then work the 2
buttonhole rows once more.
Rib 2[4:6] rows more.
Bind off in rib.

Pocket tops

Using No.2 needles and with RS facing, attach yarn to sts left on holder.
Work 6 rows K2, P2 rib.
Bind off loosely in rib.

Pullover back

Using No.2 needles and A, cast on 112[120:128] sts.
Work 56 rows K2, P2 rib.
Break off A and attach B.
Rib one row.
Break off B and attach A.
Rib 2 rows more.
Next row K twice into first st, rib 3[7:11], *pick up st between the last st worked and the next st with the left-hand needle and K or P into the back of it – called M1 – rib 7, rep from *, ending last rep with rib 3[7:11]. 129[137:145] sts.
Change to No.3 needles.
1st patt row (RS) K5, *P2, K8, P2, K9[11:13]*, rep from * to * once, P2, K8, P2, K11, rep from * to * twice more, P2, K8, P2, K5.
2nd patt row P5, *K2, P8, K2, P9[11:13]*, rep from * to * once, K2, P8, K2, P11, rep from * to * twice more, K2, P8, K2, P5.
Rep 1st and 2nd rows twice more.
7th patt row K5, *P2, slip next 4 sts onto cable needle and leave at front of work, K4, K4 from cable needle – called cable 8 – P2, K9[11:13]*, rep from * to * once, P2, cable 8, P2, K11, rep from * to * twice more, P2, cable 8, P2, K5.
8th patt row As 2nd.
Rep 1st and 2nd rows twice more.
These 12 rows form cable patt.
Continue in patt until work measures 14in from beg, ending with a WS row.

Shape armholes
Keeping patt correct, bind off 8 sts at beg of each of next 2 rows.
Dec one st at each end of every other row 10[12:14] times. 93[97:101] sts.
Continue without shaping until armholes measure 6½[7:7½]in, ending with a WS row.

Shape shoulders
Bind off 8 sts at beg of next 4 rows and 6[8:10] sts at beg of next 2 rows.
Slip rem 49 sts on holder.

Pullover front

Work as given for Back until work measures 13½in from beg, ending with a RS row (5 rows less than Back to armhole).

Shape neck and armhole
Next row Patt 64[68:72] and slip these sts on spare needle, P1 and leave this st on safety pin, patt to end.
Continue on these 64[68:72] sts for Left Front.

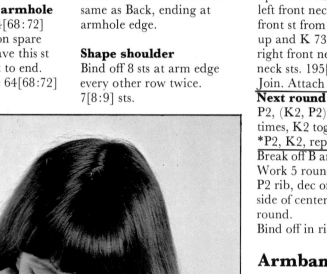

Dec one st at neck edge on next and following 3rd row. 62[66:70] sts.
Continue dec at neck edge on every 3rd row, *at the same time*, at armhole edge, bind off 8 sts on next row, then dec one st at arm edge every other row 11[13:15] times.
Continue dec one st at neck edge on every 3rd row until 23[24:25] sts rem.
Continue without shaping until armhole measures the same as Back, ending at armhole edge.

Shape shoulder
Bind off 8 sts at arm edge every other row twice. 7[8:9] sts.

Work 1 row. Bind off.
With RS facing, attach yarn to neck edge of sts on spare needle and work to end of row.
Complete to correspond to first half, reversing shaping.

Neckband

Join shoulder seams.
Using set of 4 No.2 needles, A and with RS facing, pick up and K 72[76:80] sts down left front neck, K center front st from safety pin, pick up and K 73[77:81] sts up right front neck, K 49 back neck sts. 195[203:211] sts.
Join. Attach B.
Next round Using B only, P2, (K2, P2) 17[18:19] times, K2 tog tbl, K1, K2 tog, *P2, K2, rep from * to end.
Break off B and continue in A.
Work 5 rounds more in K2, P2 rib, dec one st at each side of center front st on each round.
Bind off in rib, dec as before.

Armbands

Using No.2 needles, A and with RS facing, pick up and K 128[132:136] sts along armhole edge.
Break off A and attach B.
Work 1 row K2, P2 rib.
Break off B and attach A.
Work 5 rows K2, P2 rib.
Bind off in rib.

Finishing

Pullover. Press, omitting ribbing, on WS under a damp cloth and using a warm iron.
Join side seams.
Press seams.
Cardigan. Press as given for Pullover.
Join shoulder seams. Sew in sleeves. Join side and sleeve seams.
Slip-stitch pocket tops and linings in place.
Sew bound-off edge of collar in place around neck edge.
Fold hem to WS and slip-stitch in place.
Sew on front bands. Sew on buttons.
Press seams.
Fold ribbed cuffs in three to RS.

These needlepoint napkin rings reveal the versatility of an old design which has been adapted for a modern function. An Elizabethan pincushion inspired these rings, and the integrated pattern of strapwork and four-petaled flowers has been modified for the new design. The two flowers used, the rose and the hearts-ease, have been floral favorites in design throughout the ages.

To make the napkin rings

Materials required for making two napkin rings, each measuring 2¼ inches by 7⅛ inches before assembling:

☐ ⅛ yard double thread canvas, 27 inches wide (10 double threads to 1 inch) or ⅛ yard single thread canvas, 27 inches wide (18 threads to 1 inch)

☐ ⅛ yard lining fabric

☐ ⅛ yard interlining (optional)

☐ 1 skein of Anchor Tapisserie Yarn in each of the following colors: **Strapwork:** 0360 dark brown, 0375 ochre, 0308 gold, 0309 mustard **Roses:** 045 dark rose, 013 scarlet, 09 salmon pink **Heartsease:** 0417 dark purple, 085 cyclamen, 096 lavender **Green sepals:** 0218 dark green, 0243 parrot green, 0242 pale green

☐ Pearsall's Twisted Silk in the following colors and quantities: **Highlights and background:** 1 skein 47 yellow, 3 skeins 177 white

Alternative range of wools

☐ 1 skein of Appletons Crewel Wool in each of the following colors: **Strapwork:** Range 840 – No. 3, Range 690 – Nos. 7 and 5, Range 580 – No. 5 **Roses:** Range 220 – No. 6, No. 995, Range 500 – No. 1, Range 940 – No. 3 **Heartsease:** Range 600 – Nos. 6 and 7, Range 800 – No. 1 **Green sepals:** Range 540, Nos. 3, 5 and 8

Method of working

The strapwork and the flowers which feature in the design are worked in tent stitch in wool. Some silk is used for the highlights; the background of mosaic stitch is worked in silk. If the stitchery is worked on a double-mesh canvas (10 double threads to 1 inch), the double threads are split for working. If preferred, a single-mesh canvas can be used.

Making the napkin rings

After completing the embroidery, cut the canvas strip with seam allowances of ½ inch all around. Cut silk, velvet, felt, thin leather or any other suitable lining the same size. If the lining fabric is too fragile, it will not have the durability required of a napkin ring. If the canvas needs some slight stiffening before making up, a strip of interlining can be added. Turn in and baste seam allowances on both pieces. With wrong sides together, baste, then slip-stitch lining to canvas.

After basting the two ends of the worked canvas together to form a ring, use appropriate yarns to match the pattern exactly at the join. In this way, the join at the back of the napkin ring is scarcely visible. If desired, a fine cord can be couched down along the edges of the ring to cover the join between the worked canvas and the lining material.

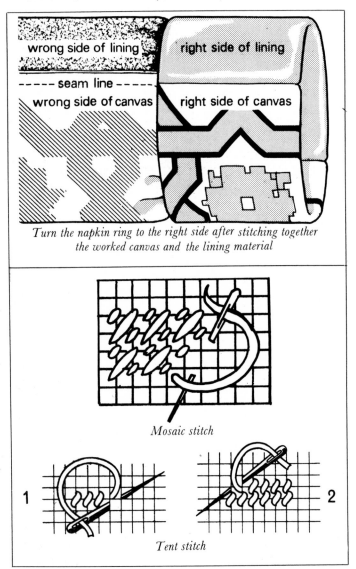

Turn the napkin ring to the right side after stitching together the worked canvas and the lining material

Mosaic stitch

Tent stitch

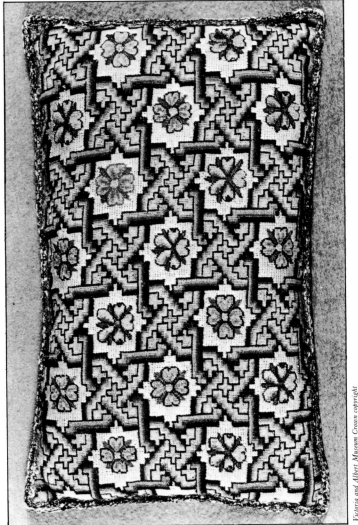

An Elizabethan pincushion, worked in about 1600, inspired the design for the napkin rings

Victoria and Albert Museum Crown copyright

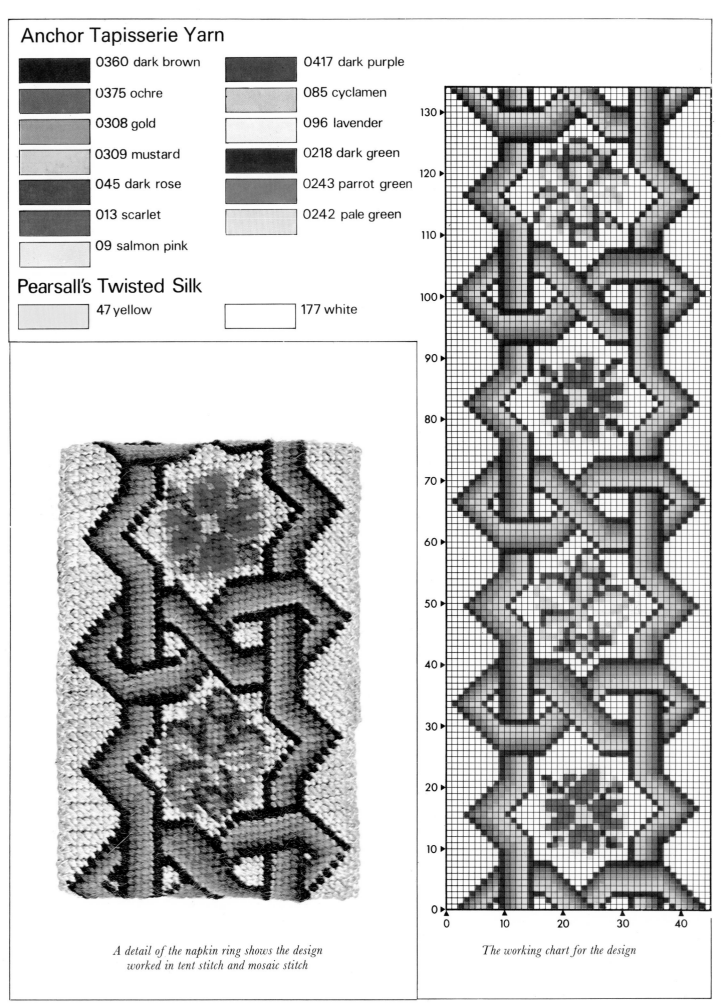

Anchor Tapisserie Yarn

0360 dark brown
0375 ochre
0308 gold
0309 mustard
045 dark rose
013 scarlet
09 salmon pink

0417 dark purple
085 cyclamen
096 lavender
0218 dark green
0243 parrot green
0242 pale green

Pearsall's Twisted Silk

47 yellow
177 white

A detail of the napkin ring shows the design worked in tent stitch and mosaic stitch

The working chart for the design

2245

Loopy coats to knit and crochet

These appealing woolly coats look attractive and make a practical cover-up for colder weather too. The jacket with its optional hood is crocheted and the cap and mittens are knitted.

Sizes
Directions are for 20in chest The figures in brackets [ ] refer to the 22in chest size
Jacket length, 12[14]in
Sleeve seam, 7½[8½]in

Gauge
Crochet. 12 sts and 12 rows to 4in over loop patt worked on No. J hook
Knitting. 5½ sts and 7½ rows to 1in over st st worked on No.5 needles

Materials
Reynolds Classique 50 grm. balls
Jacket. 3 [4] balls A, white
Hood. 1 [1] ball A, white
Cap. 1 [1] ball in each of contrasting colors B and C
Mittens. 1 [1] ball B or D, 1 [1] ball C, 1 [1] ball E
N.B. One ball only of each color will make both cap and mittens.
Jacket and Hood only. One No. J (6.00 mm) crochet hook
Jacket only. 10 [12] in. open-end zipper

Cap and Mittens only.
No. 5 knitting needles
(or Canadian No. 8)
No. 3 knitting needles
(or Canadian No. 10)

Jacket back

Using No. J hook and A
double throughout,
ch 34[38].
1st row 1sc in second ch
from hook, *1sc into next
ch, rep from * to end.
33[37] sts.
2nd row (WS) Ch 1 to count
as first sc, *insert hook into
next st, wind yarn around
one finger twice, draw loops
through, yrh and draw
through three loops, rep
from * to last st, 1sc in last st.
3rd row Ch1 to count as
first sc, *1sc into next
st, rep from * to end.
Rep last two rows until work
measures 7[8½]in from beg,
ending with a WS row.

Shape armholes
Next row Ss over first 2
sts, patt to last 2 sts, turn.
Work 1 row.
Dec one st at each end of
every other row 2[3] times.
25[27] sts.
Continue without shaping
until armhole measures 5[5½]
in, ending with a WS row.
Next row Patt over first
8 sts, turn.
Next row Dec one st, patt to
end.
Fasten off.
Skip 9[11] sts in center,
attach yarn and patt to end.
Next row Patt to within
last st, turn.
Fasten off.

Jacket left front

Using No. J hook and A
double throughout, ch18[20].
Work as given for Back to
armholes, ending with a WS
row. 17[19] sts.

Shape armhole
Next row Ss over first 2
sts, patt to end.
Work 1 row.
Dec one st at armhole edge
every other row 2[3]
times. 13[14] sts.
Continue without shaping
until armhole measures
3[3½]in, ending with a WS
row.

Shape neck
Next row Patt to last
4[5] sts, turn.
Work 1 row.
Dec one st at neck edge
every other row twice.
Continue without shaping
until armhole measures the
same as on Back, ending with
a WS row.
Fasten off.

Jacket right front

Work as given for Left
Front, reversing shapings.

Sleeves

Using No. J hook and A
double throughout,
ch21[25].
Work as given for Back, inc
one st at each end of 7th
and every following 6th row
until there are 26[30] sts.
Continue without shaping
until sleeve seam measures
7½[8½]in, ending with a WS
row.

Shape cap
Next row Ss over first 2
sts, patt to last 2 sts, turn.
Work 1 row.
Dec one st at each end of
next and every other row
until 8 sts rem. Fasten off.

Jacket neckband

Join shoulder seams.
Using No. J hook and A
double, with RS facing work
28[32] sc around neck edge,
turn.
Work 2 rows more.
If hood is not required,
fasten off.

Hood

Next row With WS facing,
work in loop patt to end,
keeping 1sc at each end of
row.
Next row Work in sc, inc
6 sts evenly across the row.
34[38] sts.
Rep last 2 rows once more.
40[44] sts.
Next row Ss over first 2
sts, patt to last 2 sts, turn.
36[40] sts.
Next row Patt to end, inc
4 sts evenly across the row.
Next row Work in patt, dec

one st at each end of row.
38[42] sts.
Rep last 2 rows once more,
then the first of them
once. 44[48] sts.
Continue without shaping
until hood measures 8[9]in,
ending with a WS row.
Fasten off.

Cap

Using No. 3 needles and C,
cast on 97[105] sts.
1st row K1, *P1, K1, rep
from * to end.
2nd row P1, *K1, P1, rep
from * to end.
Rep these two rows 2[3]
times more.
Change to No. 5 needles and
attach B.
Continue in rib, always
knitting the first row when
changing color, working
(10[12] rows B, 10[12] rows
C) twice.

Shape top
Next row Using C, K1, *K2
tog, rep from * to end.
49[53] sts.
Next row P.
Rep last 2 rows once more.
25[27] sts.
Break off yarn and thread
through sts.
Draw tight and fasten off.

Right mitten

Using No. 3 needles and C,
cast on 29[33] sts.
Work in rib as given for Cap
for 2in, ending with a
second row.
Break off C and attach E.
Change to No. 5 needles.
Continue in st st for ¾[1¼]
in, ending with a P row.

Shape thumb
Next row K19[21], turn.
Next row P4[5], turn and
cast on 4[5] sts.
Continue on these 8[10] sts
for 6 rows more.
Break off E and attach C.
Work 4[6] rows.

Shape top
Next row Continuing in C,
*K2 tog, rep from * to end.
Next row P.
Break off yarn and thread
through sts.
Draw tight and fasten off.

Join thumb seam.
Using No. 5 needles and E,
with RS facing, pick up and
K 4[5] sts along cast on sts
at base of thumb, then K to
end.
Continue in st st for 7
rows.
Break off E and attach B
or D.
Continue in st st until
work measures 4½[5½]in,
ending with a P row.

Shape top
Next row *K2 tog, K1, rep
from * to last 2[3] sts,
K2 tog, K0[1]. 19[22] sts.
Next row P.
Next row K1, *K2 tog, K1,
rep from * to end. 13[15]
sts.
Next row P.
Next row K1, *K2 tog, rep
from * to end. 7[8] sts.
Break off yarn and thread
through sts.
Draw tight.
Fasten off.

Left mitten

Work to correspond to
Right Mitten, reversing
position of thumb.

Finishing

Jacket. Sew in sleeves,
join side and sleeve seams.
If worked, join top of hood.
Press all seams lightly
under a damp cloth, using a
warm iron.
Using No. J hook, work
2 rows sc along each front
edge and around front of
hood.
Sew in zipper.
Press.
Cap. Join seam.
To make a loopy pompon,
take a piece of cardboard
about 6in wide and using B
and C together, wind about
20 times around the
cardboard. Slip loops off
cardboard and tie firmly
around the center. Sew to
top of cap, spreading loops
all around.
Mittens. Join seams.
Press seams.

Wild flower motif

A floral motif is always popular on household linen, and this brightly colored sprig of wild flowers is particularly suitable for working on a crisp linen tablecloth. To make an attractive matching set, place one small flower from the design in the corner of each of a set of linen napkins. Or, give a fresh look to linen guest towels, sheets and pillow cases by embroidering them with this delicate floral design, either centered on the fabric or worked in one corner.

Materials required to work the motif

☐ D.M.C. 6-Strand Floss in the following colors: 817 turkey red, 796 cobalt blue, 809 light cobalt blue, 725 amber gold, 435 cinnamon, black, 3053 light gray-green; 3051 gray-green

☐ No. 9 embroidery or crewel needle

Method of working

Trace the design onto the background fabric using dressmakers' carbon paper. Using three strands of floss, work the flowers and the leaves in satin stitch, and the stems in stem stitch.

▲ *Tracing pattern for working the motif on smaller items*
▼ *A range of household linens is suitable for the embroidery*

The wild flowers are worked in satin stitch and stem stitch

▼*Enlarged tracing pattern for working the embroidery on a tablecloth*   ▲ *Adapt the motif for a tablecloth and matching linen napkins*

FASHION CROCHET

Flower bolero

The rows of flowers making up this unusual bolero are individual crocheted motifs. The motifs are worked in three different sizes, then stitched together to create this attractive design. The bolero is finished off with a criss-cross front lacing.

Size

Directions are for 24in chest
Length to shoulder, 14in

Gauge

Each small flower measures 1½in diameter

Materials

Reynolds Classique
50 grm. balls
1 ball each of 5 colors,
A, B, C, D and E
One No. E (3.50 mm)
crochet hook

Motifs

Small flower

Using No.E hook and A, ch 8. Join with ss to first ch to form circle.
1st round Ch1, work 11sc into circle, join with ss to first ch. 12 sts.
2nd round Ch2, 2dc into same st as ss, (1sc into next st, 3dc in next st) 5 times, 1sc in next st, join with ss to second of ch2.

Fasten off, leaving a 6in end for sewing.
Make 78 more motifs in the same manner using A, 34 in B, 34 in C, 32 in D and 28 in E.

Medium flower

Using No. E hook and D, work first two rounds as given for Small Flower.
3rd round *Ch3, work 1sc behind sc of last round by inserting hook from back of work into sp before sc, take hook around sc and out again at back and finish as for sc, rep from * 5 times more, ending with ss into first of ch3.
4th round Ss into first ch3

loop, ch2, 4dc into this loop, *1sc in next sc, 5dc in next loop, rep from * 4 times more, 1sc in last st, join with ss into same place as ss of 3rd round.
Fasten off, leaving a 6in end for sewing.
Make one more motif in the same manner using D, and two more in E.

Large flower

Using No. E hook and C, work first four rounds as given for Medium Flower.
5th round As 3rd.
6th round As 4th, but working 7dc into each loop instead of 5dc. Fasten off, leaving a 6in end for sewing.

Make one more motif in the same manner using C and two more in E.

Finishing

Press each piece very lightly under a damp cloth, using a warm iron and taking care not to flatten the flowers. Join the motifs as shown in the diagram, and when joining medium or large flowers, do so at the back of the first round so that they take up the same space as a small flower.
Using A, make a twisted cord and thread it through the centers of the motifs at the edge of the bolero, to tie.

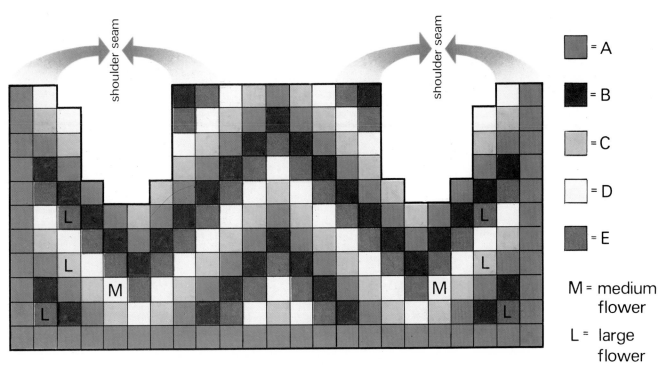

shoulder seam

shoulder seam

= A

= B

= C

= D

= E

M = medium flower

L = large flower

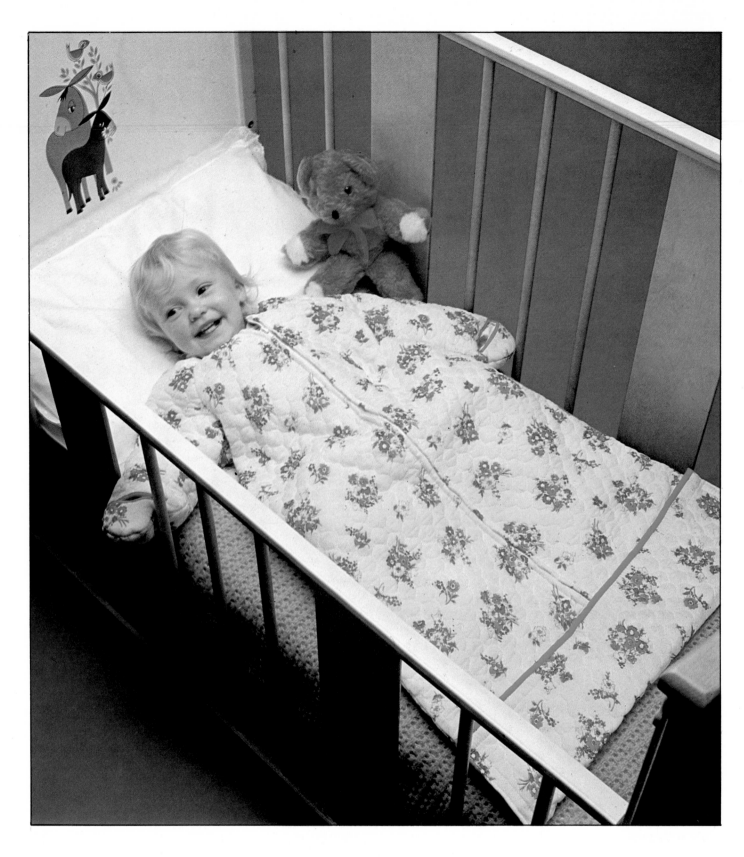

HOME SEWING

Baby's sleeping bag

Made up in washable quilted nylon fabric, this snugly shaped sleeping bag is attractive and practical. The sleeves have slit openings for the baby's hands, and the lower half of the sleeping bag has enough room to insure complete freedom of movement. When the toddler stage is reached the bottom flap can be removed to form a cozy bath robe.

Materials you will need:

☐ 2 yards 36 inch wide quilted fabric
☐ 2 yards 36 inch wide cotton or Dacron lawn
☐ 1 inch wide binding to tone with fabric
☐ ¾ yard ⅝ inch wide Velcro
☐ 26 inch open-ended nylon zipper

To make the sleeves

Draw up the pattern pieces from the graph given here, on which one square equals one square inch. Cut one sleeve front and sleeve back and then reverse the pattern pieces to cut the second.

Make a slash in each sleeve as indicated on the pattern. For each sleeve cut two 2 inch wide pieces of binding to the length of the opening plus 1½ inches. Place the trim on the right side of the fabric with the edges meeting along the line of the opening. Baste in position (Fig. 1). Working on the right side stitch the binding to the fabric along each side of the opening ⅛ inch from the slit, and extend the stitching ½ inch beyond the slit at each end, overstitching the ends to secure (Fig. 2). Remove the basting.

Working on the wrong side, cut miters at the corners of the opening ½ inch deep, taking care not to cut the trim (Fig. 3). Pull the trim through the opening to the wrong side, and press the miters and trim away from the opening.

Working on the right side, stab stitch along the trimming seam line (Fig. 4). On the wrong side, work an oversewing stitch at each end of the opening to hold the facing in position.

To make the sleeping bag

With right sides together, pin and baste the left sleeve front to the left jacket front, matching notches. Stitch, taking a ¼ inch seam allowance, which is given throughout the pattern. Clip the curve and press the seam open, using a cool iron. Repeat for the right side.

Stitch the right and left sleeve backs to the jacket back, matching notches. With right sides together, join the two halves of the sleeping bag along the side seams, matching notches.

Cut the lining for the sleeping bag, using the same pattern pieces as above. Make up in exactly the same way as the quilted fabric, but omit slashing the sleeve fronts, and keep the stitching just within the seam line so that the lining is slightly smaller than the quilted bag. Trim the seams and press open.

With wrong sides together, insert the lining in the quilted jacket. With the lining facing out, baste around the seams, the lower edges of the sleeves and around the neck edge, to hold the lining in place.

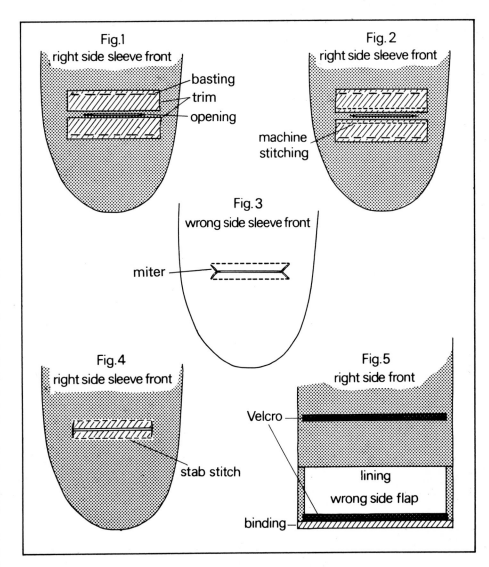

Fig.1 right side sleeve front — basting — trim — opening

Fig.2 right side sleeve front — machine stitching

Fig.3 wrong side sleeve front — miter

Fig.4 right side sleeve front — stab stitch

Fig.5 right side front — Velcro — lining — wrong side flap — binding

Turn the sleeping bag right side out. Slash the lining to the same width as the opening for the hand. Turn to the wrong side and turn under ¼ inch on the raw edge of the lining and hem neatly to the binding on the wrong side of the opening.

To insert the zipper

Press the seam allowance for the front opening on the quilted fabric to the wrong side. Place the zipper in position, baste and stitch, making sure not to catch the lining. Turn under the seam allowance on the lining to the wrong side, press and slip-stitch neatly to each side of the zipper.

Machine stitch ¼ inch in from the neck edge of the jacket to secure the lining to the quilted fabric. Cut a length of binding the length of the neck edge. Pin and baste the binding to the neck of the jacket ¼ inch from the edge, and stitch along the seam line. Turn the binding to the wrong side and slip-stitch neatly in place.

To make the flap

Trim ½ inch off the hem on the quilted

jacket front, taking care not to cut the lining. Bring the lining to the right side to cover the raw edge of the quilted fabric and baste in place. Cut a length of Velcro the width of the jacket front and place one piece in position to cover the edge of the lining. Baste and stitch the Velcro in place.

Cut a length of binding the width of the lower edge of the jacket back, which forms the flap. Place the binding in position on the right side of the flap, overlapping the edge by ½ inch. Baste and stitch. Turn the binding to the wrong side and baste in place. Place the second piece of the Velcro in position on the wrong side of the flap so that it lies over the raw edge of the binding (Fig. 5). Baste in place and stitch.

Fold the raw edges of quilted fabric along the sides of the flap to the wrong side to make neat. Baste.

Turn under the raw edges of the lining and slip-stitch to make neat.

To convert the sleeping bag into a robe for an older baby, simply cut off the flap to the same length as the jacket front and bind the raw edges.

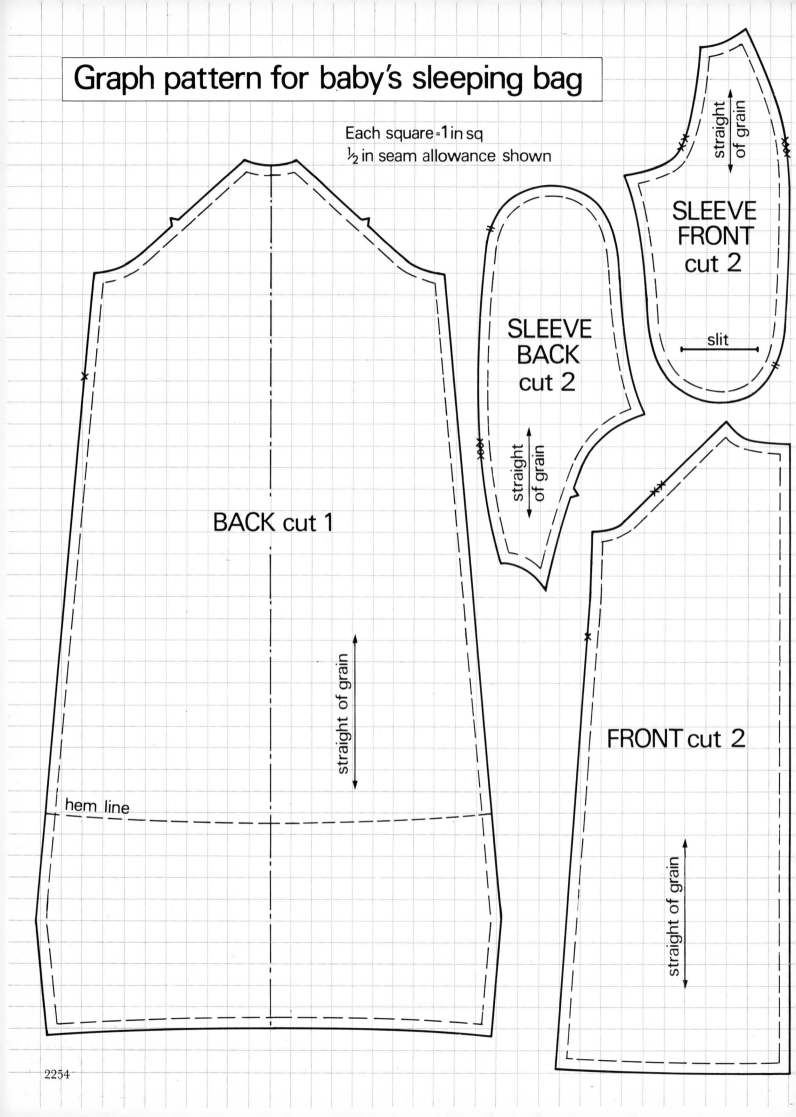

Graph pattern for baby's sleeping bag

Each square = 1 in sq
½ in seam allowance shown

SLEEVE
FRONT
cut 2

straight of grain

slit

SLEEVE
BACK
cut 2

straight of grain

BACK cut 1

straight of grain

hem line

FRONT cut 2

straight of grain

2254

SEW EASY
Curves
of color

This eye-catching evening coat is designed to team up with the evening dress featured on page 2260. The coat is made in nylon shantung and the decoration takes the form of bands of vividly contrasting colors worked as a reverse facing.

The coat is relatively easy to make, providing that care is taken with the placing of the layered facings.

Fabrics and notions

For the evening coat in all sizes you will need:

- [ ] 36 inch wide fabric: 4 yards main color; $1\frac{1}{8}$ yards contrast 1; $1\frac{3}{8}$ yards contrast 2; $1\frac{1}{2}$ yards contrast 3 and $1\frac{3}{4}$ yards contrast 4
- [ ] sewing thread to match main fabric
- [ ] machine embroidery thread to match each contrasting fabric
- [ ] machine embroidery thread to contrast with each contrasting fabric
- [ ] graph paper for making pattern

The pattern

The pattern is given in sizes 10, 12, 14 and 16. Draw up the pattern pieces from the graph, on which each square represents 1 square inch. No seam allowances are included on the pattern, so add $\frac{5}{8}$ inch to all edges when cutting out. Cut a pattern for each contrasting facing piece and mark it with the appropriate number.

Cutting out

Cut out the front, back and sleeves from the main fabric color, following the pattern layout. Cut a facing in each of the contrasting colors following the layout for facings.

To make the coat

Seams

1. With wrong sides together, baste and stitch the front shoulder dart. Press the dart flat toward the center front.

2. With wrong sides together, baste and stitch the shoulder seam. Press the seams open.

3. With wrong sides together, baste the side seams from the underarm to the lower notch and stitch the width of the machine foot away from the raw edge. Trim the seam and press it flat.

Turn the coat to the wrong side and work a second row of stitching the width of the machine foot from the stitched edge, to form a French seam. Snip the seam allowance in to the end of the stitching at the notch.

With wrong sides together, baste and stitch the seam from the notch to the hem to form a plain seam. Press the seam open.

The seams and darts will be covered by the contrasting facings when the coat is completed.

Sleeve facings

4. With the wrong side of the fabric uppermost, assemble the contrasting facing pieces in the order shown.

Baste along the lower edge of each strip $\frac{5}{8}$ inch from the raw edge. These basting lines indicate the lower edge of each colored band.

5. Place the right side of the facing to wrong side of the sleeve, baste and stitch to within $\frac{5}{8}$ inch of the sleeve edge at each end. Press the seam open. Grade the seam and turn the work to the right side. Baste along the fold edge and press.

6. Lay the sleeve flat on the table and pin and baste the layered facing carefully in position on the sleeve along the top of each band.

7. Using French chalk, draw by hand the wavy pattern lines on each of the different colored strips of facing.

Use the two sets of basting lines on each

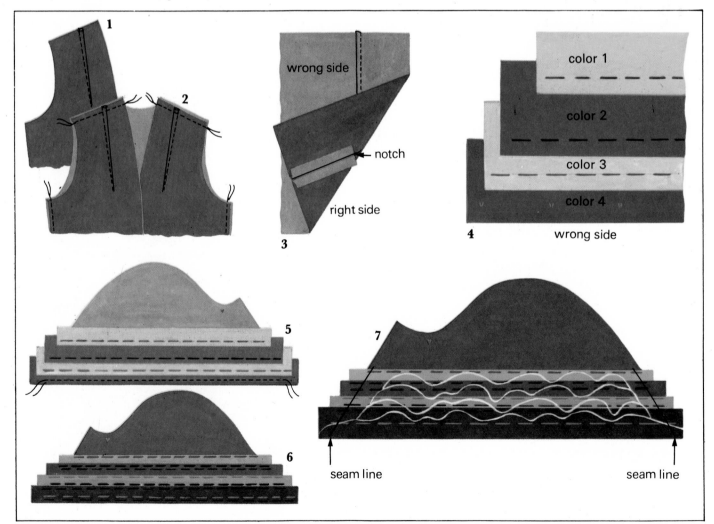

band as a guide to the depth of the pattern on the top three bands. On color 4, finish the pattern line at least 1 inch inside the sleeve seam line.

8. Using a narrow zigzag stitch setting on the machine, and matching thread, stitch along the pattern lines to within 1 inch of the sleeve seam line at each end.

9. Using a pair of sharp embroidery scissors, trim away the surplus fabric on the facings, cutting as close as possible to the stitching lines, but taking care not to trim beyond the lines of stitching.

Using machine embroidery threads in a contrasting color and a wider, closer zigzag setting, stitch over the trimmed design edge. Again, only stitch color 4 to within 1 inch of the sleeve seam line, leaving the end of the band loose. This will allow the necessary freedom to stitch the sleeve seam. The embroidery for this section is completed after the sleeve seam has been closed.

10. Run two rows of gathering threads around the sleeve head.

With wrong sides together, stitch the sleeve seams as instructed for the side seams of the coat, working the French seam from the underarm to the lower notch on the sleeve and a plain seam from the notch to the sleeve hem edge.

11. Overlap the remaining loose ends of color 4, and baste in place. Complete the zigzag stitching, running the top overlap line down to the sleeve point to cover the join.

Front and back coat facings

Assemble each of the other sets of facings (left front, right front, back hem and back neck), as instructed for the sleeve facings.

Do not attempt to join the facings together at this stage; it is easier to overlap each color as required when the facings are ready to be basted onto the garment.

12. Place the right side of the facing to the wrong side of the garment, baste the facings in the correct positions, overlapping the color 4 bands where they join. Stitch around the entire edge. Clip the curves where necessary, turn and press the seam.

13. Lay the facings flat on the garment and baste each layer in position, overlapping the bands where they join. (These joins should, when embroidered, form an integral part of the completed design.)

The facings should be layered carefully over the bust dart and basted in position, absorbing the extra fullness in the design of the completed appliqué.

Draw on the design lines, taking the line down to meet the next color band where the joins occur. Stitch, trim and embroider as instructed for the sleeves.

Note: It is much easier to handle the garment without the sleeves sewn in, so it is advisable to complete all the embroidery with the exception of color 1, over the armhole seam, before the sleeves are sewn in.

Make sure that the edge of the color 2 band does not touch the seam at the shoulder head.

Sewing in the sleeve

14. With right sides together, matching balance marks and easing in the fullness, baste and stitch the sleeve into the armhole with the sleeve uppermost.

Make neat the armhole seam by working a second row of stitching the width of the machine foot away from the first. Trim the excess fabric to the stitching line and overcast the raw edge. Press the seam toward the sleeve.

Baste down and complete color 1 appliqué to cover the seam at the shoulder head.

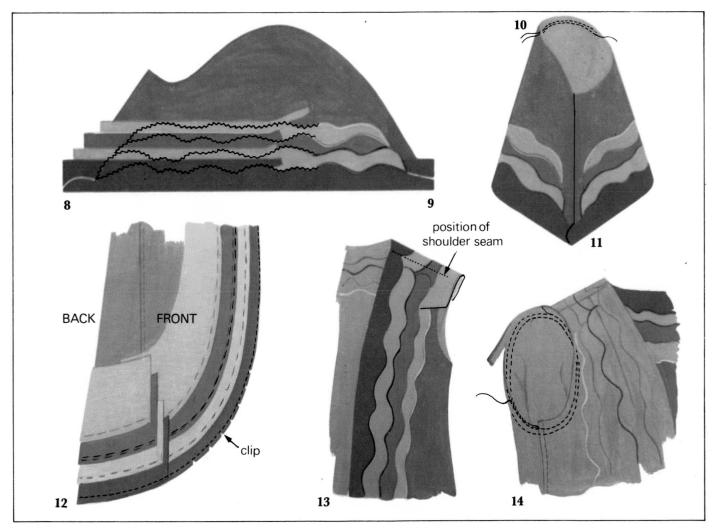

8   9   10

11

BACK   FRONT

position of shoulder seam

clip

12   13   14

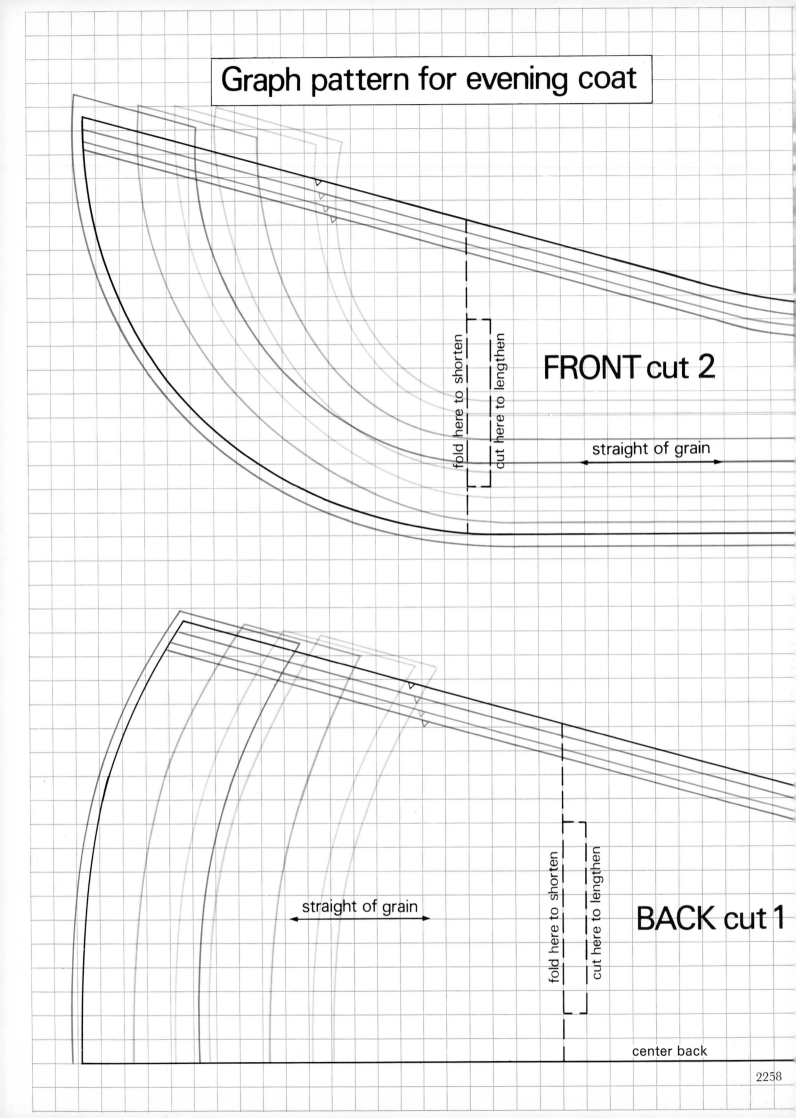

Graph pattern for evening coat

FRONT cut 2

fold here to shorten

cut here to lengthen

straight of grain

BACK cut 1

straight of grain

fold here to shorten

cut here to lengthen

center back

2258

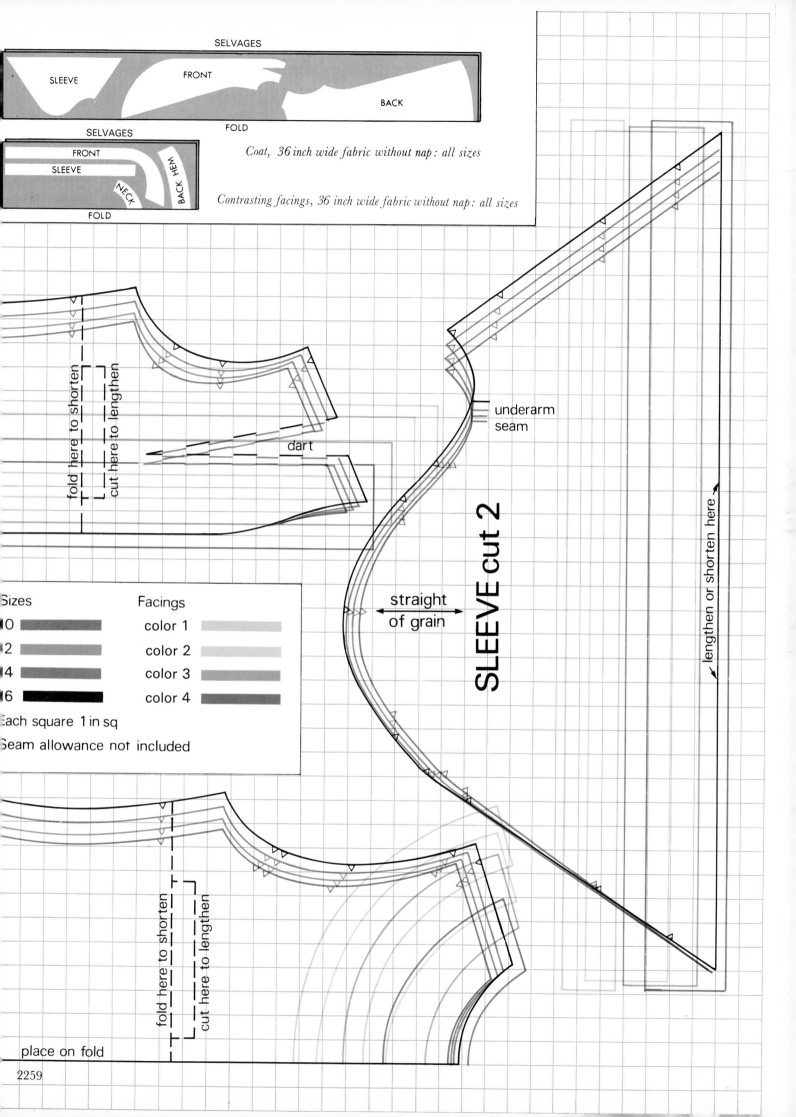

SELVAGES

SLEEVE FRONT

BACK

FOLD

Coat, 36 inch wide fabric without nap: all sizes

SELVAGES

FRONT
SLEEVE
BACK HEM
NECK

FOLD

Contrasting facings, 36 inch wide fabric without nap: all sizes

fold here to shorten
cut here to lengthen

dart

underarm
seam

SLEEVE cut 2

straight
of grain

lengthen or shorten here

Sizes		Facings	
0		color 1	
2		color 2	
4		color 3	
6		color 4	

Each square 1 in sq

Seam allowance not included

fold here to shorten
cut here to lengthen

place on fold

2259

QUICK MAKE
Elegance in jersey

Team this elegant evening dress with the evening coat featured on page 2255. The pattern for the dress is designed for use with lightweight jersey fabrics only, as it depends on the stretch of the fabric for ease.

for ease.

The dress is cut very small as it is important that the bodice and sleeves fit closely. The tight-fitting bodice contrasting with the fluid lines of the skirt is a major feature of the design. To display the drape of the fabric to the best effect, the cut also allows extra length.

Fabrics and notions

For this evening dress you will need:
- [ ] 36 inch wide jersey fabric, 6½ yards for sizes 10 and 12; 6¼ yards for sizes 14 and 16
- [ ] sewing thread to match fabric
- [ ] graph paper for pattern

The pattern

The pattern given here is to fit sizes 10 and 12, 14 and 16. The back length measurement from 2 inches below the normal neckline to the hemline is 56½ inches.

Draw up the pattern pieces from the graph given here, on which one square equals one square inch. No seam allowances are included on the pattern, so remember to add ⅝ inch to all edges when cutting out the pattern pieces.

From the remaining fabric, cut long lengths on the bias, each 1½ inches wide, for making the rouleau bound edges on the neck, sleeve and hem edges of the dress.

To make the dress

Finish all the seams by working a second row of stitching the width of the machine foot away from the first row. Trim the excess fabric close to the machine stitching and either overcast the raw edge by hand, or machine stitch to make neat.

1. With right sides together, baste and stitch the front piecing to each side of the dress front. Make neat the seam edge and press flat away from the center front.

2. With right sides together, baste and stitch the center back seam. Make neat the seam edge and press it flat.

3. With right sides together, matching notches and easing in the fullness between the notches, baste and stitch the side seams of the dress. Make neat the seam and press flat toward the back.

4. Work a row of stay stitching around the wrist edge of the sleeve.

With right sides together, baste and stitch the sleeve seam. Make neat the seam edge and press flat toward the back.

5. With right sides together, baste and stitch the sleevehead dart. Make neat the seam and press flat toward the back.

6. With right sides together, matching notches and underarm seams, baste and stitch the sleeve into the armhole with the sleeve uppermost. Make neat the seam edges and press toward the sleeve.

7. Work a row of stay stitching around the neckline of the dress to prevent it from stretching out of shape.

Hang the dress up for 24 hours to allow the hem to drop.

Try on the dress and mark the hemline. Join the bias cut strips to make the required length. Fold the bias strip in half lengthwise and carefully press the folded edge by placing the iron on it one section at a time.

8. With right sides together, pin, baste and stitch the double raw edge of the rouleau along the sleeve edge, taking care to make a sharp point over the hand. Fold over the double edge and slip-stitch to the line of stitching as shown.

9. Make two 3 inch long rouleau strips, twist them into loops and attach them to the point on the sleeve hem edge to slip over the finger when worn.

10. With right sides together, baste and stitch the double raw edge of the rouleau around the neck edge and finish as described for the sleeve edge.

11. With right sides together, baste and stitch the double raw edge of the rouleau around the dress hem edge by hand, using small running stitches. The skirt hem is cut on the bias and will stretch out of shape if it is machine stitched. Press lightly.

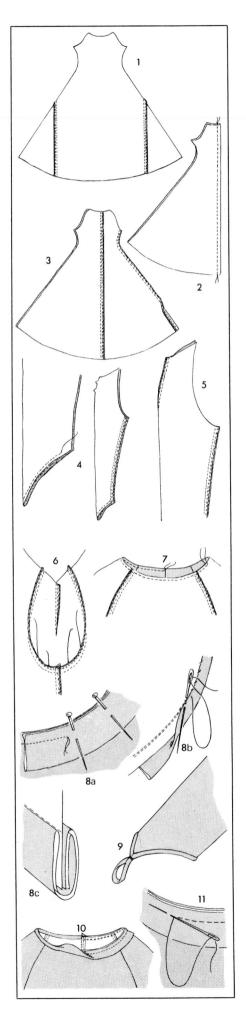

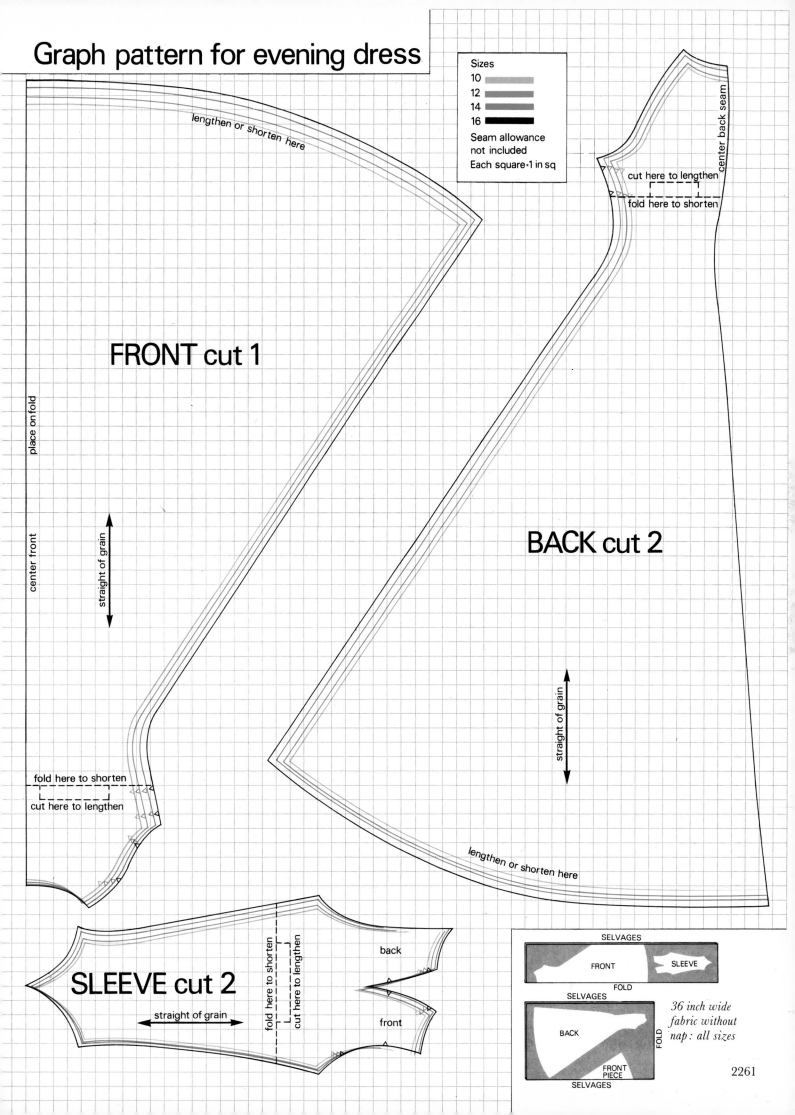

Graph pattern for evening dress

Sizes
10
12
14
16

Seam allowance not included

Each square = 1 in sq

lengthen or shorten here

FRONT cut 1

place on fold

center front

straight of grain

fold here to shorten

cut here to lengthen

SLEEVE cut 2

straight of grain

fold here to shorten

cut here to lengthen

back

front

cut here to lengthen

fold here to shorten

center back seam

BACK cut 2

straight of grain

lengthen or shorten here

SELVAGES

FRONT

SLEEVE

FOLD

SELVAGES

SELVAGES

BACK

FOLD

FRONT PIECE

SELVAGES

36 inch wide fabric without nap : all sizes

2261

Pinafore with a pocket

Any little girl would love this pretty pinafore with an embroidered hen nesting comfortably on the pocket. And it makes a useful cover-up to wear over skirts, dresses and pants, especially when made up in a tough washable cotton. We chose a light fabric but the colors can be varied according to choice and the embroidered motif would be just as effective on a yellow or navy background.

To make the pinafore

Materials required for the pinafore (size 6 as shown):

- ☐ $\frac{2}{3}$ yard 45 inch wide (or $\frac{3}{4}$ yard 36 inch wide) cotton gabardine
- ☐ 4 yards bias binding
- ☐ 1 skein of D.M.C. 6-Strand Floss in each of the following colors: 606 flame, 347 geranium, 921 orange, 783 amber gold, 782 dark amber gold, 704 spring green, 912 emerald, 910 dark emerald
- ☐ 4 buttons

Making the pocket

Mark the outline of the pocket shape on the fabric but do not cut it out until the embroidery has been completed. Trace the design onto the pocket and work the embroidery according to the colors and stitches indicated in the diagram.

The main outline of the hen is worked in stem stitch using six strands of floss in the needle. The rest of the design is worked in satin stitch, chain (and detached chain) stitch, backstitch, fly stitch and French knots. Vary the number of strands for working each area as seems most suitable.

Cut out the pocket after completing the embroidery, allowing $\frac{1}{4}$ inch turnings all around. Bind all the edges with bias binding.

Making the pinafore

Cut out the pinafore pieces from the cotton gabardine, using the graph pattern given. Allow $\frac{3}{8}$ inch turnings at the shoulder and side seams only and use French seams when sewing up. Fold back the center back facings and bind all around the pinafore at the neck, hem and back (over the double thickness of fabric). Bind the armholes. Make the buttonholes at the center back and sew on the buttons. Position the pocket on the front of the pinafore, baste and stitch in place.

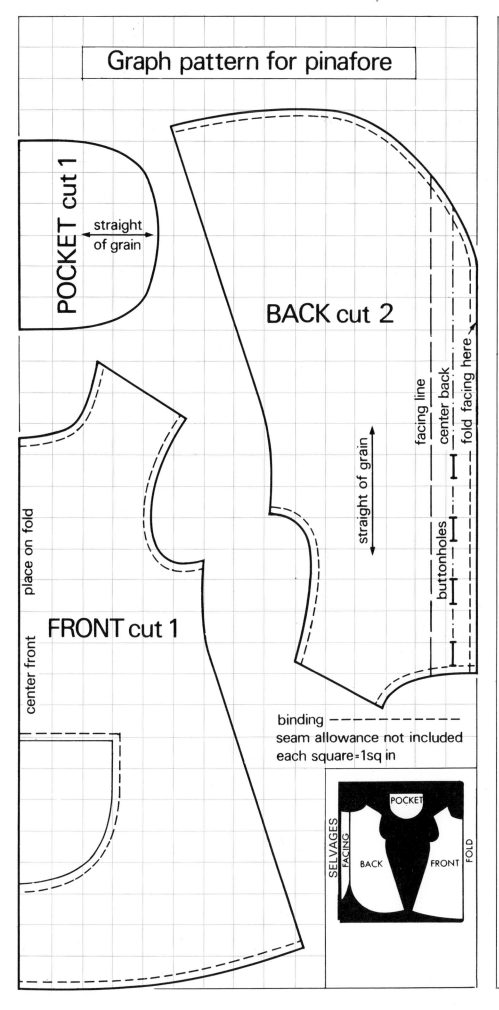

Graph pattern for pinafore

POCKET cut 1

straight of grain

BACK cut 2

facing line

center back

fold facing here

straight of grain

buttonholes

FRONT cut 1

place on fold

center front

binding — — — —
seam allowance not included
each square = 1 sq in

SELVAGES

FACING

POCKET

BACK

FRONT

FOLD

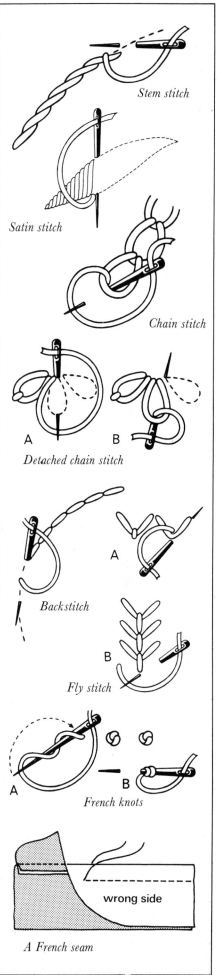

Stem stitch

Satin stitch

Chain stitch

A   B

Detached chain stitch

A

Backstitch

B

Fly stitch

A   B

French knots

wrong side

A French seam

2263

Tracing pattern

KEY

colors

- 347 geranium
- 606 flame
- 921 orange
- 783 amber gold
- 782 dark amber gold
- 704 spring green
- 912 emerald
- 910 dark emerald

stitches

- satin stitch
- stem stitch
- chain stitch
- detached chain stitch
- backstitch
- French knots
- fly stitch

2264

A row of small people to sew. This family of cheerful little rag dolls is made from one basic pattern. The dolls' clothes are also simple to make following the patterns given here, and they can be easily elaborated and adapted to suit particular play requirements.

For each doll you will need:

- ☐ 12 inch by 12 inch piece of cotton fabric
- ☐ Kapok for stuffing
- ☐ embroidery thread in pink and black, for features
- ☐ scraps of left-over fabric, ribbon and braid for clothes
- ☐ narrow elastic
- ☐ hooks and eyes
- ☐ elastic thread

To make the doll

Draw up the basic doll pattern pieces from the graph pattern given here, in which one square equals one inch.

With right sides together, baste and stitch the two sections taking $\frac{1}{4}$ inch seam allowance and leaving 2 inches open at the top of the head for turning and stuffing. Clip curves, turn to the right side. Stuff the doll firmly and overcast the opening to close.

Work the eyes on each doll in satin stitch, using black embroidery thread. For the girl dolls add stitched eyelashes, worked above or below the eye. Work a curved line in stem stitch, using pink embroidery thread, to form the mouth of the boy dolls. Work a satin stitched Cupid's bow in pink embroidery thread for the girl dolls. Use a felt-tipped pen to make freckles and round pink cheeks. To make the hair, use the balls from ball fringe stitched firmly in place, or thread a large needle with sports yarn and make large loops all over the head, or take a thick skein of sports yarn, backstitch it down the center to give the effect of a parting, and braid it at each side of the doll's head.

To make the clothes

Girl with black choker

Draw up the dress pattern piece from the graph pattern. Cut out two from flowered fabric. Cut one dress piece down the line indicated on the pattern piece. For the sleeve frills, cut two lengths of flowered fabric 7 inches by 1 inch. With right sides together, stitch the dress side seams. Run a line of gathering stitches down one long side of each sleeve frill, draw up to fit the armholes. Baste and stitch in place. Stitch the back seam, leaving open a length long enough for the dress to be slipped over the doll's head. Stitch a hook and eye at the neck edge to close. Turn the dress to the right side and fit it on the doll. Draw up the pants pattern piece and cut it out from white cotton fabric. With right sides together, stitch the pants pieces together across the crotch and down the side seams. Turn the pants to the right side and add a trimming of narrow lace around the legs. Turn a narrow hem at the waist edge and insert a length of elastic. Stitch three small black beads down the front of the dress bodice. Thread beads on strong thread to make a choker. Finish off the doll with a bow of black ribbon in her hair.

Girl with vest

Draw up the basic bodice pattern from the graph. Cut out from white cotton fabric. Cut one bodice piece down the line indicated on the pattern. With wrong sides together, stitch the side and sleeve seams. Turn to the right side and add an eyelet embroidery trim at neck and cuffs. Stitch a hook and eye at the neck edge to secure. Draw up the basic vest pattern from the graph. Cut out from purple felt.

Cut one vest piece along the line indicated on the pattern piece. Stitch shoulder and side seams. Stitch pink braid around the vest and armhole edges.

To make the skirt, cut a piece of flowered fabric 7 inches by 1 inch for the waistband, a piece 17 inches by 5 inches for the main skirt piece, and a piece 28 inches by 1 inch for the ruffle. Run a line of gathering stitches along one long edge of the ruffle piece, and draw up to fit the skirt edge. With right sides together, baste and stitch. Run a line of gathering stitches along the top edge of the skirt and draw up to fit the waistband. With right sides together, baste and stitch the waistband to the skirt. Fold the waistband over and slip-stitch on the wrong side. Stitch the back seam, leaving an opening large enough for the skirt to be fitted on the doll. Stitch a hook and eye in position to close.

Finish off the doll with a small artificial flower in the hair and another flower stitched to the vest.

Girl with mob cap

Cut out the bodice pieces, cutting them short across the dotted line indicated on the pattern. Make the bodice as above, gathering the sleeves at the wrist edge. Cut a strip of fabric 1 inch by 20 inches long and gather one long edge to fit the bodice neck. With right sides together, baste and stitch in place. Make the ruffled skirt as described above, omitting the waistband. With right sides together, baste and stitch the skirt to the bodice. Stitch a hook and eye at the back neck opening of the bodice.

To make the mob cap, cut a $5\frac{1}{2}$ inch diameter circle of flowered fabric. Turn a narrow hem around the edge of the circle. Run two rows of elastic thread $\frac{3}{4}$ inch and 1 inch from the edge of the circle, and draw up to fit the doll's head. Stitch a large artificial flower on the hat brim and a smaller flower on the bodice front.

Boy in blue suit

Cut out the jacket from the basic bodice pattern and make in dark blue fabric as described above. Cut a strip of blue fabric 7 inches by 1 inch and, wrong sides together, stitch it to the neck edge. Turn the strip over to the wrong side and slip-stitch in position to form a stand-up collar. Stitch orange rickrack braid around the neck, cuffs and jacket hem. Cut three small circles of orange felt and stick in position down the front of the jacket to represent buttons. Stitch a hook and eye at the back neck opening to secure. Draw up the basic trouser pattern from the graph, and cut out from the dark blue fabric. Join center seams and then inside and outside leg seams. Turn a narrow hem at the waist edge and insert elastic. Draw up to fit doll and secure. Stitch a trimming of orange rickrack around the bottom of each leg to finish off.

Boy in red suit

Make the bodice in green fabric, and edge the cuffs with red and green braid. Make up the vest in red fabric, and stitch red and green braid around the vest and armhole edges. Make the trousers in red fabric, and add a green buttonhole-stitched patch at the knee. Finish the doll off with a scarf of red ribbon or tape.

Boy in purple shorts

Make the bodice in red fabric. Cut the sleeves short, and add buttons cut from green felt. Cut a tiny pocket and stitch in place on the shirt, adding a triangle of green felt for a handkerchief. Make the bodice in green fabric, and edge the basic trousers pattern and cutting the legs short across the dotted line indicated on the pattern. Cut two strips of purple fabric each 6 inches by 1 inch. Fold in half longitudinally and stitch. Stitch the straps to the shorts, placing them so that they cross over at the back.

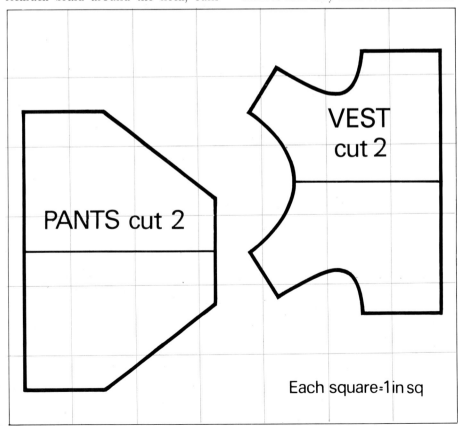

PANTS cut 2

VEST cut 2

Each square=1 in sq

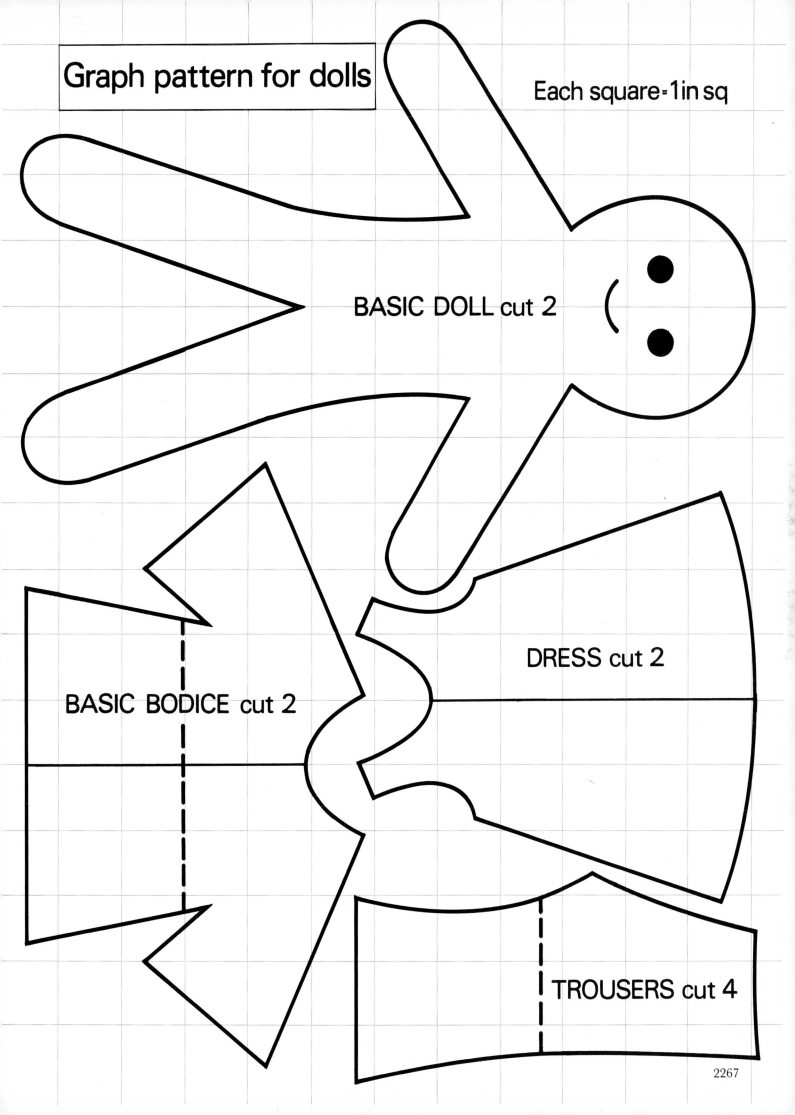

Graph pattern for dolls

Each square = 1 in sq

BASIC DOLL cut 2

DRESS cut 2

BASIC BODICE cut 2

TROUSERS cut 4

2267

KNITTING FOR WOMEN

Jumper dress

This knitted jumper dress is specially designed to be slimming on the fuller figure. It is worked in a soft yarn to give a smooth surface and the overlap is positioned off-center to create a slenderizing effect

Sizes

Directions are for 38in bust
The figures in [] refer to the 40:42:44in bust
Length from shoulder, 39[39½:40:40½]in

Gauge

6 sts and 8 rows to 1in over st st worked on No. 5 needles

Materials

Columbia Minerva Nantuk Sport Yarn
7 [7:8:8] 2 oz. skeins
One pair No. 3 knitting needles (or Canadian No. 10)
One pair No. 5 knitting needles (or Canadian No. 8)
One No. 3 circular needle, 24 in. long
11 buttons

Back

Using No. 3 needles, cast on 152[158:164:170] sts.
Work 6 rows g st.
Change to No. 5 needles.
Work 14 rows st st, beg with a K row.
Next row K1, sl 1, K1, psso, K to last 3 sts, K2 tog, K1.
Continue without shaping for 7 rows more.
Rep last 8 rows 13 times more. 124[130:136:142] sts.
Continue dec in this manner at each end of next and every following 6th row until 102[108:114:120] sts rem.
Continue without shaping for 5 rows more, ending with a P row.
Change to No. 3 needles.
Work 4 rows g st.

Change to No. 5 needles.
Continue in st st, beg with a K row, inc one st at each end of 5th and every following 6th row until there are 116[122:128:134] sts.
Work 9 rows more or until work measures 31½in from beg, ending with a P row.

Shape armholes
Bind off 10 sts at beg of each of next 2 rows. 96 [102:108:114] sts.
Next row K1, K2 tog, K to last 3 sts, sl 1, K1, psso, K1.
Next row P.
Rep last 2 rows 7[8:9:10] times more. 80[84:88:92] sts.

Shape neck
Next row K30[31:32:33], turn and slip rem sts on extra needle.
Next row P1, P2 tog, P to end.
Next row K to last 3 sts, K2 tog, K1.
Rep last 2 rows 7 times more. 14[15:16:17] sts.
Continue without shaping until armhole measures 7½[8:8½:9]in, ending at neck edge.

Shape shoulder
1st row P to last 5 sts turn.
2nd row Sl 1, K to end.
3rd row P to last 10 sts, turn.
4th row as 2nd.
Slip sts on holder.
Return to sts on extra needle, leave first 20[22:24:26] sts on holder, attach yarn to next st.
Next row K1, sl 1, K1, psso, K to end.
Next row P to last 3 sts, P2 tog tbl, P1.
Complete to correspond to first side, reversing shaping as shown.

Front

Right side
Using No. 3 needles, cast on 90[93:96:99] sts.
Work 6 rows g st.
Change to No. 5 needles.
1st row K.
2nd row P73[76:79:82], P2 tog, turn.
3rd and every other row Sl 1, K to end.
4th row P75[78:81:84], P2 tog, turn.

6th row P77[80:83:86], P2 tog, turn.
Continue in this manner, working 2 sts more on every other row until:
12th row P83[86:89:92], P2 tog. 84[87:90:93] sts.
Break off yarn and slip these sts on an extra needle.

Left side
Using No. 3 needles, cast on 73[76:79:82] sts.
Work 6 rows g st.
Change to No. 5 needles.
Work 2 rows st st, beg with a K row.
3rd row K56[59:62:65], sl 1, K1, psso, turn.
4th and every other row Sl 1, P to end.
5th row K58[61:64:67], sl 1, K1, psso, turn.
Continue in this manner, working 2 sts more on every other row until:
13th row K66[69:72:75], sl 1, K1, psso, cast on one st, then K across sts of Right side. 152[158:164:170] sts.
14th row P84[87:90:93], K1, P to end.
Working the cast-on st as P on RS rows and K on WS rows, continue as given for Back from ** to end.

Neckband

Weave shoulder seams tog by positioning the two sets of sts on needles one behind the other, WS tog.
Insert threaded darning needle into first st on front needle as if to P and draw yarn through, leaving st on needle. *Insert darning needle into first st on back knitting needle as if to P it and slip it off the needle, then insert darning needle into next st on back needle as if to K, leave on knitting needle but draw yarn through. Insert darning needle into first st on front knitting needle as if to K and sl off knitting needle, then insert darning needle into next st on front needle as if to P, leaving it on knitting needle and pulling yarn through. Rep from * until all sts have been worked off.
Using No. 3 circular needle and with RS facing, beg at

right shoulder, * pick up and K 22[25:28:31] sts down straight edge of neck, 16 sts down shaped edge, K sts from holder, pick up and K 16 sts up shaped edge and 22[25:28:31] sts up straight edge of neck to shoulder, rep from * around front neck. 192[208:224:240] sts.
Continue in g st.
1st round P.
2nd round *K21[24:27:30], K2 tog, K14, K2 tog, K18[20:22:24], K2 tog, K14, K2 tog, K21[24:27:30], rep from * once more.
3rd round P.
4th round *K20[23:26:29], K2 tog, K14, K2 tog, K16[18:20:22], K2 tog, K14, K2 tog, K20[23:26:29], rep from * once more.
Bind off as to P.

Armbands

Using No. 3 needles and with RS facing, pick up and K 120[126:132:138] sts around armhole.
Work 4 rows g st.
Bind off as to K.

Front border

Using No. 3 circular needle, beg at lower edge and pick up and K one st in each st up the line of P sts on Front, then pick up and K 3 sts along same line over Neckband.
Work 6 rows g st.
Bind off as to K.

Finishing

Press work under a damp cloth, using a warm iron.
Join side seams.
Sew end of front border to end of border on Right front edge at bottom curve. Sew the end of the left front border under the right front border at this point.
Press seams.
Sew on buttons, the top one on neckband, one on line of g st at waist, the bottom one to the joining of borders at bottom curve and positioning two more between top and waist buttons and six more between waist and bottom buttons.

Knit and Crochet Abbreviations

In pattern instructions for both knitting and crochet it is usual for a shortened form to be used for the most common terms. Here we give a list of the abbreviations you are likely to find in Creative Hands.

alt	=	alternate
beg	=	beginning
ch	=	chain
cl	=	cluster
cm	=	centimeter
dc	=	double crochet
dec	=	decrease
dtr	=	double treble
gr(s)	=	group(s)
grm(s)	=	gram(s)
hdc	=	half double
in	=	inch(es)
inc	=	increase
K	=	knit
K-wise	=	knitwise
KB	=	knit into back of stitch
M1K	=	make 1 knitwise by picking up loop between stitch just worked and following stitch and knit into the back of it
M1P	=	make 1 purlwise by picking up loop between stitch just worked and following stitch and purling into the back of it
No.	=	number
P	=	purl
P-wise	=	purlwise
patt	=	pattern
PB	=	purl into back of stitch
psso	=	pass slip stitch over
rem	=	remaining
rep	=	repeat
RS	=	right side
sc	=	single crochet
sl 1	=	slip 1 knitwise
sl 1P	=	slip 1 purlwise
sp(s)	=	space(s)
sl st	=	slip stitch in knitting
ss	=	slip stitch in crochet
st(s)	=	stitch(es)
st st	=	stocking stitch
tbl	=	through back of loop(s)
tog	=	together
tr	=	treble crochet
TW2	=	twist 2 by knitting into front of 2nd stitch then front of first stitch on left-hand needle and slipping 2 stitches off needle together
TW2B	=	twist 2 back by knitting into back of 2nd stitch then back of first stitch on left-hand needle and slipping 2 stitches off needle together
WS	=	wrong side
ytb	=	yarn to back
ytf	=	yarn to front
yoh	=	yarn over hook
yon	=	yarn over needle

ADVANCED
DRESSMAKING

Sewing
with sheers

The soft feminine look in fashion could well be with us for several seasons and apart from lingerie and nightwear, sheer fabrics are very much part of the fashion scene. There are many different types of sheers ranging from soft fabrics to very stiff ones.

They are so fine and dainty that the usual dressmaking methods are too clumsy to use and new ones must be learned. Because these fabrics are see-through, seam allowances show on the right side as do the usual interfacings and the whole sewing approach has to be changed. The methods used, however, are not so much difficult as different.

Pattern, fabrics notions

Choosing the pattern

Select a pattern with fullness and soft flowing lines, preferably with a skirt cut on the straight of grain. Bias cut skirts in these fabrics tend to drop badly. If the skirt has a pronounced flare, it is wise to hang it for 24 hours to drop before marking the hem finally.

Very full sleeves look particularly good in sheer fabric. Take care when choosing a pattern with a full sleeve, for one that looks generous in a thicker fabric may look skimpy in a very fine one.

As these fabrics are fragile it is best to avoid a tight fitting bodice or tight sleeves. If the pattern you wish to make does have a fitted bodice you can interline the bodice and combine it with full unlined sleeves. This way will also solve the problem of what to wear underneath.

1. If you have chosen a garment with front buttoning and a front facing seam, eliminate the seam by cutting the facing in one with the bodice as shown.

Inter- or underlining

A mounted interlining is often used with sheer fabrics on those areas you wish to be opaque. Here interlining and top fabric are basted together before stitching, and the two fabrics are sewn as one.

Unlike a separate lining, there has to be a perfect marriage between lining and interlining fabric, therefore the correct combination is important. Use a soft natural fiber interlining with a natural fiber top fabric, such as a soft Japanese silk.

A synthetic underlining should only be used with a synthetic top fabric, otherwise you cannot work the outside fabric properly. For instance when pressing,

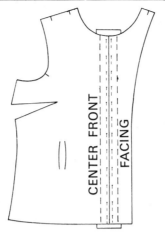

1. *Combined front and front facing*

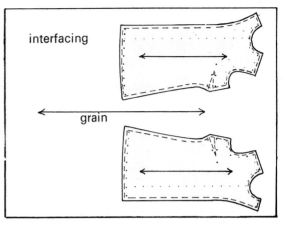

2. *Cutting out the interlining*

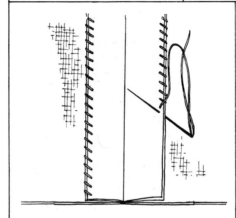

3. *Overcasting interlined seam allowances*

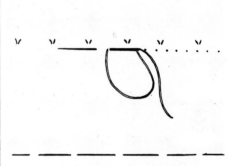

4. *Prick stitching just below hemline on interlined garment*

the outside fabric may require greater heat than the lining can withstand.

Alternatively, if you are after a translucent effect, use a double layer of the top fabric if it is plain. Or, if patterned, mount with a similar but matching plain fabric.

Cutting out: cut out top fabric and mark details. Place pieces to be underlined singly onto single interlining fabric. Make sure that the grain lines match exactly and take care not to stretch the fabric.

2. Baste all around each piece within the seam allowance or darts to avoid marking the fabric.

Cut out and work top fabric and interlining as one.

Seams. Seams in mounted fabrics are stitched as usual and not as for unmounted sheers.

3. When finishing off the raw seam allowances it is most important that they are overcast by hand. A machine finish on a mounted fabric tends to curl the two layers, creating a thick and hard seam edge which makes an impression through the fabric on the outside.

4. To prevent the interlining from folding up inside a hem, prick stitch fabric and interlining together just below the hemline before the hem is turned up. When sewing up the hem do not sew through to the outside fabric, but catch the interlining fabric only to give the outside a smooth finish.

Interfacing

Interfacing of the usual type will be too heavy for sheer fabrics. Use either a lining fabric or a pure silk organza as interfacing. Pure silk organza is so colorless it can be used for most transparent fabrics.

If you still find that the interfacing shows through and changes the color of the fabric it is best to leave it out, provided the fabric has enough substance to support itself.

Notions

Thread: use a fine thread for sewing sheers.

Needles and pins: these should be very fine. Use dressmaker's silk pins or glass head pins. Glass head pins are made from needle discards and are good with fine fabric.

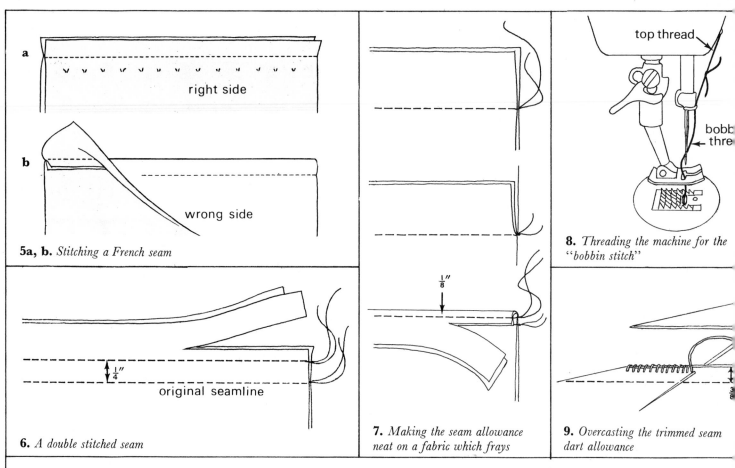

5a, b. *Stitching a French seam*

6. *A double stitched seam*

7. *Making the seam allowance neat on a fabric which frays*

8. *Threading the machine for the "bobbin stitch"*

9. *Overcasting the trimmed seam dart allowance*

Working the fabric

Cutting out

If the selvage is tight, snip it at 4 inch intervals.

As the fabric is slippery it is a good idea to lay it out on a sheet.

Take care not to stretch the fabric when folding and laying it out.

Use fine pins and pin the pattern down at frequent intervals. When cutting out, hold the fabric securely with your free hand.

Tailor's tacks are best for marking pattern details as chalk and carbon markings are difficult to remove on these fabrics.

Machine stitching

Use a new fine needle on the machine and a fine thread. Test the machine for pressure, stitch length and tension on a double piece of fabric before starting on the garment.

If you find that the fabric puckers as you stitch it, place the fabric over tissue paper when stitching. The paper can easily be torn away afterward.

Seams

There are several alternatives for stitching the seams on sheer fabrics. The object being to combine a strong seam, for a fabric which frays, with a narrow neat seam allowance, as this is visible from the right side of the garment.

A French seam is often used on fine fabrics but is only suitable if the seam is straight. To make a French seam work as follows:

5a. With wrong sides together, machine stitch $\frac{1}{4}$ inch from seamline in seam allowance. Trim as close to stitching line as possible and press the seam allowance to one side.

5b. Turn the garment to the wrong side. With right sides together stitch along the original seamline, encasing the raw edges in the seam.

Decide if you wish to use French seams before you start basting a garment for fitting. If you do, then baste as in **5a** and pin along the seamline.

Double stitching (**6**). Stitch along the seamline, with right sides together. Make another row of stitching in the seam allowance through both layers, $\frac{1}{4}$ inch from the first row. Trim seam allowance to $\frac{1}{8}$ inch from second row.

Fraying fabrics: if your fabric frays badly here are two good ways of dealing with the seam allowance. Stitch the seam on the seamline with right sides together. Trim seam allowance to $\frac{3}{8}$ inch and finely overcast the edges together.

7. Alternatively, after you have stitched the seam, press the seam allowance to one side. Fold under the seam allowance $\frac{1}{8}$ inch from the stitching line and stitch through fold with a straight stitch or zigzag. Trim as close to the second line as possible.

Darts

To avoid a knot or backstitch showing at the point of a dart, sew the dart by the "bobbin stitch" method.

Thread the machine as usual except for the needle.

8. Draw the bobbin thread through the hole in the needle plate as usual then thread it through the needle, reversing the threading order you would use with the top thread. Knot the two threads together as shown.

Pull the bobbin thread until it is twice the length of the dart plus 2 to 3 inches, then wind the spool of thread until the slack is taken up.

Stitch the dart starting at the point. If the fabric does not fray, rethread the needle in the same way and work another row of stitches $\frac{1}{4}$ inch from the first. Trim close to this line.

9. Alternatively, trim the dart seam allowance to $\frac{3}{8}$ inch and overcast the raw edges very finely together.

Armhole seams

Here are two good ways to finish the armhole seam:

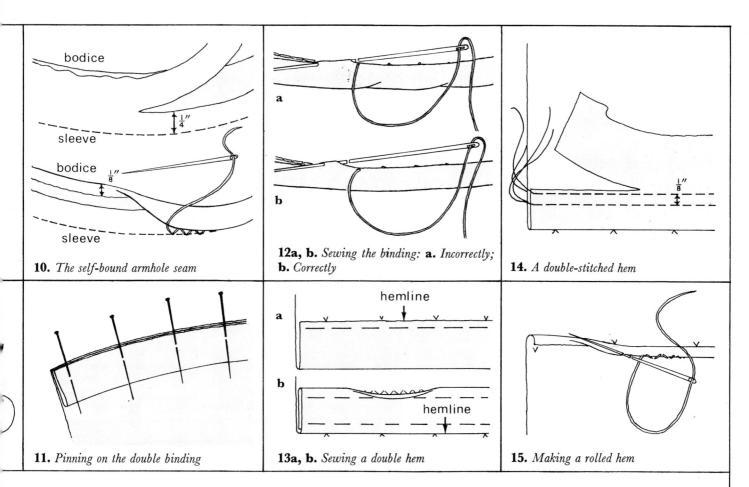

10. *The self-bound armhole seam*

12a, b. *Sewing the binding:* **a.** *Incorrectly;* **b.** *Correctly*

14. *A double-stitched hem*

11. *Pinning on the double binding*

13a, b. *Sewing a double hem*

15. *Making a rolled hem*

Trim the armhole seam allowances to a $\frac{3}{8}$ inch and overcast finely.

10. Alternatively the armhole seam can be self bound. Stitch the armhole seam along the seamline in the usual way. Trim seam allowance of sleeve only to $\frac{1}{4}$ inch. Fold bodice seam allowance under $\frac{1}{8}$ inch. Place fold to seamline and slip stitch loosely to machine stitches thus covering the sleeve seam.

Bound edges

Binding is a particularly good way to finish a neck edge if you do not want a bulky facing finish. A double binding is much easier to work on a fine fabric than a single one.

Here is how to work a double binding. It is a good idea to experiment on the width before working on the garment itself.

Decide on the width you would like the finished binding. Cut strips of bias fabric to the required length and slightly more than 6 times the width of the finished binding.

Fold strip in half lengthwise, wrong sides together, and press carefully along the folded edge by placing the iron on it section by section. (You will find that the fabric stretches a bit and loses some of its width.)

11. Trim off the seam allowance of the edge to be bound. With right sides to-

gether, pin the double raw edge to the trimmed seam edge. As sheer fabrics often have a tendency to stretch, work very carefully, resting the work on a flat surface.

After pinning, baste in place with a fine thread and small stitches.

Machine stitch, taking a seam allowance which is $\frac{1}{3}$ of the width of the folded strip.

Remove the basting. With the work still resting on a flat surface, bring the folded bias edge over the seam allowance onto the seamline. Pin.

12a, b. Using a fine thread hand sew as shown. Do not tighten the stitches. Never insert the needle into the fabric for a new stitch exactly opposite the end of the previous one (**a**) but insert it a grain or two further on (**b**).

Hem

If your hem edge is straight and you want to make the usual type of hem, it is a good idea to make it double.

13a, b. To do this fold the raw edge up to the hemline and baste (**a**). Fold again, on hemline, and baste (**b**). Stitch very neatly with an invisible hemming stitch.

14. An alternative hem finish, suitable for any type of hem, is to turn it up on the hem edge and stitch with two rows of stitches about $\frac{1}{8}$ inch apart.

Trim off seam allowance close to top row of stitches.

Hand rolled hem

Another way of finishing the hem edge is to hand roll it. Here are two ways of doing this, try both first on a scrap of fabric to see which you have more success with.

15. Trim the seam allowance to $\frac{1}{4}$ inch. Rolling the edge a few inches at a time between thumb and forefinger, first turn under $\frac{1}{8}$ inch then roll up a further $\frac{1}{8}$ inch and slip stitch in place to complete the roll. The slip stitches should be closely placed to hold the roll firmly, but make sure that the stitches don't show on either side. Take a single thread for each stitch.

The second method is to stitch a line of machine stitching in the hem allowance $\frac{1}{4}$ inch from the hemline. Trim close to this, then proceed as before.

Fastenings

Avoid heavy buttons or zippers as these can drag and distort the fabric and are quite out of character with very light-weight sheers.

Try light-weight buttons with loops or tiny buttonholes as these will give a fine delicate finish appropriate to the fabric. Use hooks and eyes and small snap fasteners for hidden fastenings.

ADVANCED DRESSMAKING

Cutting a raglan sleeve

Fashion trends show the emergence of a softer line. One way to achieve this is with the raglan sleeve. If the pattern you want to use is right in all details except for the sleeve, here's how to convert a simple set-in sleeve to a raglan.

Preparing the pattern

Requirements

The pattern must have a simple bodice and plain set-in sleeves, without any shoulder detail and preferably with a high round neck. Before working on the pattern, trim all seam allowances from it.

Patterns with contour bodice seaming are not suitable.

You will need a ruler, pencil, red crayon or felt tip pen, some large sheets of tracing paper and clear tape.

Choosing the style

1a, b. You will need to decide on the depth of the raglan. You can have a simple raglan which runs into the original sleeve underarm line (**a**) or an extra deep raglan (**b**).

2a, b, c. If you are making a simple raglan you have a choice of sleeve line which can alter the appearance of your shoulder width. There is the raglan shape (**a**) or you can make the shoulders look wider (**b**) or narrower (**c**).

Back shoulder dart

A back shoulder dart has to be swung into the back neck before you cut the raglan sleeve.

3. Draw a line from the center of the neck as shown. Cut along the line.

4. Close up the original dart. The cut opens up to form the new dart which should be drawn as shown.

Underarm bust darts

If the pattern front has an underarm bust dart it is usually best to swing this in to a front body dart. You can, if you wish, keep the underarm dart on the simple raglan version.

Mark the position of your bust point on the pattern. To do this measure the length from your shoulder to bust point and the distance from the center front to bust point.

5. Extend the bust dart to the bust point as shown.

6. If the pattern already has a front body dart also extend that to the bust point as shown. Cut out the front body dart along these lines.

7. If the pattern does not have a body dart draw a line from bust point to waist and cut along this line.

8. Close the bust dart and stick a piece of paper behind the body dart that has opened up.

9. Draw in the new dart as shown: do not take it right up to the bust point as darts should never run right on to the bust.

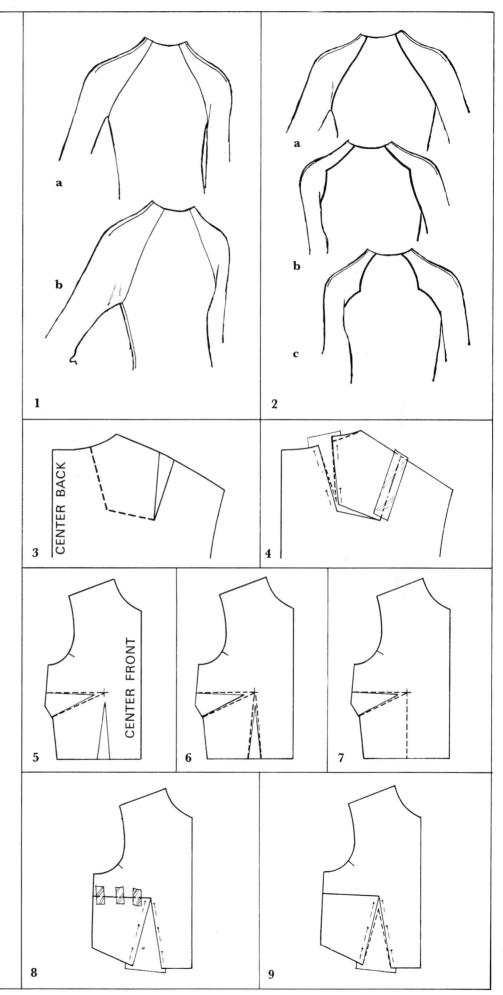

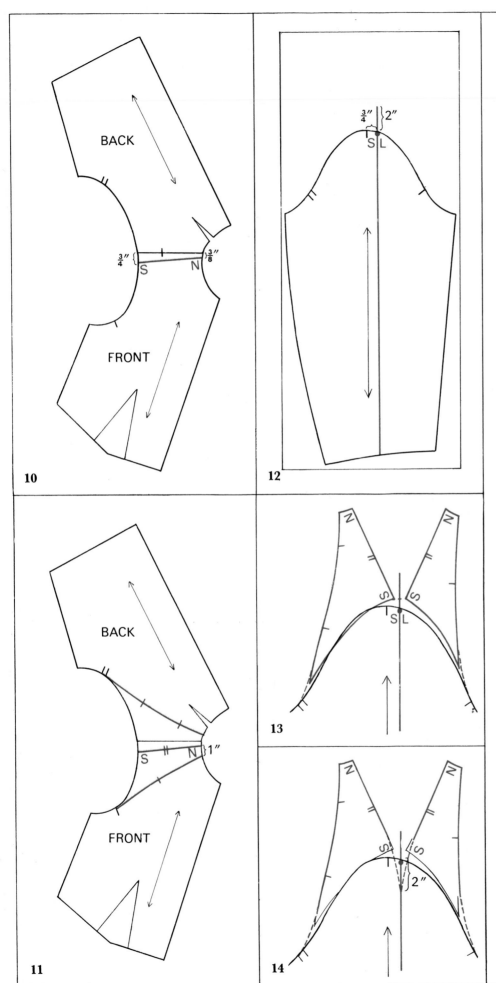

10

11

12

13

14

Simple raglan

10. Lay the bodice patterns out flat with the shoulder seams corresponding. Draw new shoulder line on front $\frac{3}{8}$ inch down at neck and $\frac{3}{4}$ inch down at shoulder. Mark the new shoulder line N at neck edge and S at shoulder.

11. Outline the shape of the raglan. This line usually starts 1 inch each side of N and goes down to the notches on the armhole. Mark the line in red and put in balance marks.

Lay a large sheet of tracing paper over the pattern. If the tracing paper is not large enough to cover the pattern stick pieces together with clear tape.

Trace off the back, front and raglan sections, mark the raglan lines, the new shoulder line and put in the balance marks, grain lines and darts. Label each piece clearly.

Cut out the patterns along the outside lines and the raglan lines.

12. Make a tracing of the sleeve pattern, leaving 8 inches of tracing paper clear above the crown. Trace off all sleeve markings such as darts, grain lines and balance marks.

To compensate for the alteration of the shoulder line on the bodice pattern, move the shoulder point $\frac{3}{4}$ inch to the front. Mark this point SL.

Draw a line parallel to the grain line through SL and extend the line for 2 inches above the crown.

Cut the raglan section along the new shoulder line NS to separate the front raglan section from the back raglan section.

13. Using these sections place the shoulder points S $\frac{1}{2}$ inch above SL and $\frac{1}{4}$ inch to each side of the extended line, with the armhole edge to the back and front crown line, as shown.

14. Draw all around new raglan line, curving gently into sleeve at armhole edge. Extend into the original sleeve head over the top of the sleeve head for 2 inches to give a smooth narrow dart over the top of the arm.

Transfer balance marks, grain lines and darts to tracing. Cut out sleeve pattern. This gives a pattern without seam allowances, so mark this fact on all pattern pieces and remember to add $\frac{5}{8}$ inch all around when cutting out.

Having made the pattern it is a good idea to make it up in muslin or other cotton to check the fit before cutting into your fabric.

Deep raglan sleeves

First prepare the pattern as before, cutting off seam allowances and swinging underarm and shoulder darts.

Set up the pattern as for a simple raglan and draw in a new shoulder line (figure **10**).

15. Draw in the raglan line. This line should not be more than $1\frac{1}{2}$ inches to each side of N and not deeper than 2 inches below the armhole point. Mark the lines in red and put in balance marks.

Lay a large sheet of tracing paper over the pattern. If the tracing paper is not large enough to cover the pattern stick pieces together with clear tape. Trace off the back, front and raglan sections. Mark the raglan lines, the new shoulder line and put in the balance marks, grain lines and darts. Label each piece clearly.

Make a tracing of the sleeve pattern, leaving 8 inches of tracing paper clear above the crown. Trace off all sleeve markings such as darts, grain lines and balance marks.

Find the point SL as in figure **12**, and draw the line parallel to the grain line through this point as before.

16. Cut the raglan section along the new shoulder line to separate the front raglan section from the back raglan section.

Place the raglan pieces $\frac{1}{2}$ inch above SL and $\frac{1}{4}$ inch each side of extended line. Slash into raglan pieces as shown and spread close to crown line. Allow the under-armhole point to extend 2 inches at back and front.

Join the new point to the elbow line in a gentle curve as shown.

17. Draw all around the new raglan line, curving into the sleeve and curving into the top of the sleeve head for 2 inches to give a smooth narrow dart over the top of the arm.

Transfer balance marks, grain lines and darts to tracing. Cut out sleeve pattern.

You can either make a one piece sleeve following the outline or cut down the broken line illustrated and make a two piece sleeve. If you separate the pattern, name each piece carefully.

This gives a pattern without seam allowances, so mark this fact on all pattern pieces and remember to add $\frac{5}{8}$ inch all around when cutting out.

Having made the pattern it is a good idea to make it up in muslin or other cotton to check the fit before cutting into your fabric.

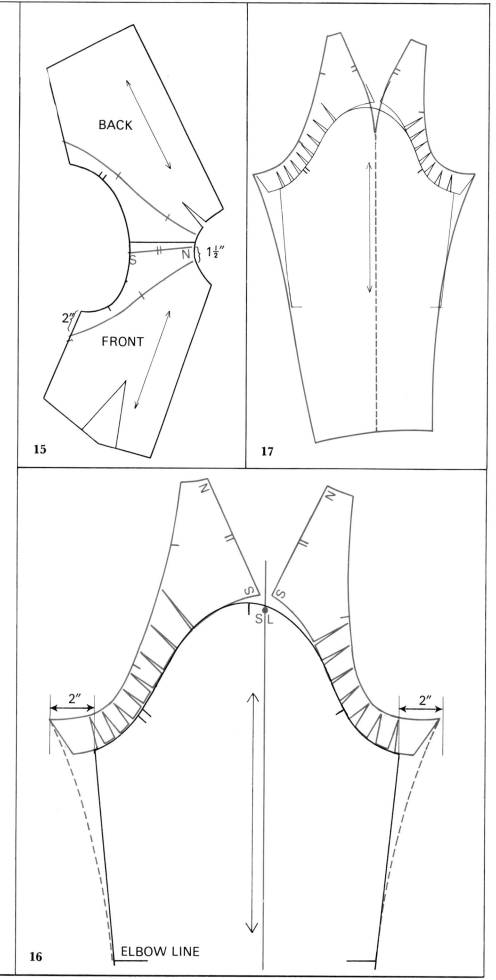

ADVANCED DRESSMAKING

short cuts to an expert finish

One of the secrets of enjoyable dressmaking is to make your every day clothes quickly, and to keep ambitious intricate patterns for special occasion wear. Here are a few labor saving ideas which will save time but still give very good results.

Cuffs, tab fastenings, both genuine and false, and a simulated, but most effective, bound pocket are dealt with here.

Make your dressmaking more adventurous by substituting these simple methods for the more complicated ones generally given with commercial paper patterns.

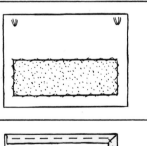

1

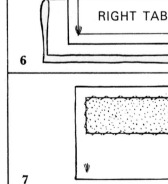

← hand circumference plus 1″ →

FOLD

twice cuff depth plus ½″

2

FOLD

baste

3

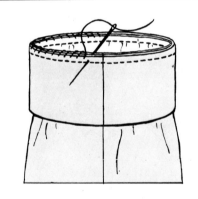

4

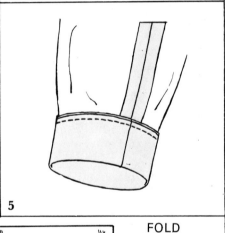

5

Cuffs

Here is a cuff without an opening or sleeve placket, which is suitable for stretch fabrics such as jersey.

The method of attaching this cuff to the sleeve is far less bulky than the usual method, as all seam allowances are pressed toward the sleeve. You will find it has other uses too, such as stitching a cuff onto a short puff sleeve made of a bulky fabric.

1. Since this cuff has no opening you will need to be able to put your hand through the closed cuff. Measure the circumference of hand at the knuckles to include the thumb.

2. Cut the cuff to the length of this measurement plus 1 inch and to twice the required width plus ½ inch.

Join the narrow edges of each band, with right sides facing and taking ½ inch seam allowance. Press seam open.

3. Fold band in half, wrong sides together, and baste ½ inch from raw edges.

Sew sleeve seam, make neat and press. Trim the wrist seam allowance to $\frac{1}{4}$ inch.

4. Place right side of cuff to right side of sleeve with seams matching. Stitch in place, taking $\frac{1}{4}$ inch seam allowance. Overcast or zigzag edge to make neat.

5. Fold cuff down with seam allowances into sleeve. Press lightly.

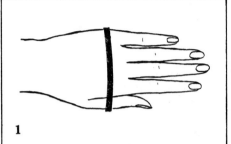

RIGHT TAB   LEFT TAB

FOLD

grain

6

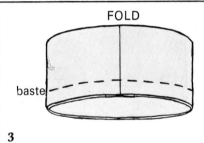

snip

A

7

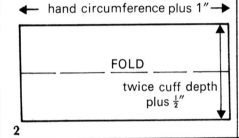

NECK

NECK

8

Tab openings

Occasionally one side of a tab opening stretches during the making. By cutting on a fold and being careful to keep the grain absolutely straight, the danger can be minimized.

6. Cut the right- and left-hand tabs with the outside seamline on a fold.

7. Cut interfacings without turnings and catch stitch to the wrong side of the top section of each tab piece. Snip to point A as shown.

8. Press back all seam allowances except at the neck edge, mitering corners neatly and cutting away spare fabric if there is too much bulk. Baste.

9. Fold tabs in half and press.

10. Cut opening in bodice as shown in your pattern, then stay stitch and snip as illustrated.

11. Slip bodice between right-hand tab, matching points carefully. Baste and top stitch.

12. Fold right tab forward and attach left-hand tab in the same way.

13. Fold tabs into correct position and hem at back.

Tab opening with shirt collar

If the tab opening is associated with a shirt type collar, proceed as before up to diagram 8 inclusive, then fold tabs right sides together and stitch along the neck seam for the distance shown in the pattern instructions.

14a, b. Snip into the seam allowance as illustrated (**a**) then turn (**b**). Finish as above.

False tab

Many people find a plain neckline too severe and unflattering. The use of a false or mock tab provides a quick solution; it will break up the plain front and so lessen the severe effect, and is very easy to make without a pattern. Alternatively, a false tab can also be used to replace a functional tab on a pattern.

15. Cut out a tab with ½ inch seam allowances.

16. Turn under the seam allowance, snipping curves or mitering corners where necessary.

17. If you want to make buttonholes in the tab do so now.

18. Place the tab centrally at the neck. Baste and topstitch in place.

Substituting a false tab

You can substitute a mock tab for a real one on the pattern if you wish, but if you do, remember not to cut a front opening as given on the pattern. Remember also that you will need to add a neck opening down the center back.

19. If the pattern has a collar you will have to make the collar in two pieces, adding a seam allowance to the center back of the collar.

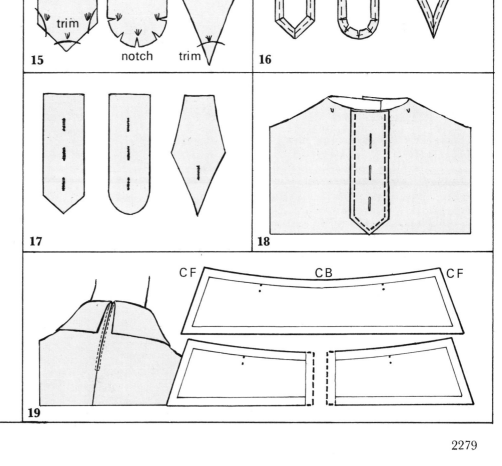

Simulated bound pocket

If you are not too happy about making pockets, try this one, but only if your fabric has a firm weave and will not fray. This type of bound pocket looks especially good on a muslin or denim jacket.

20. Baste around the pocket shape as given in the pattern. This varies with style but the average size of a bound pocket is 6 inches by $\frac{1}{2}$ inch. Cut a piece of iron-on interfacing 2 inches wider and 2 inches longer than the opening and iron this centrally to the wrong side.

21. Working from the front cut the pocket opening as shown.

22. Turn cut edges to back, making sure that you follow the basting lines. Press and remove basting.

Cut two strips of fabric to the pocket length plus 2 inches and 2 inches wide. You can use self or contrasting fabric. Cut two pieces of double sided interfacing to the same length as the strips and 1 inch wide.

23. Iron this to one half of each strip.

Remove the interfacing backing, fold strip in half along the length and press.

24. Lay the strips to the back of the pocket, with the folds meeting along the center of the opening. Pin in place. Turn to right side and check that the folds really are central before basting firmly.

25. Working on the right side top stitch carefully, $\frac{1}{8}$ inch from opening edges.

For the pocket bag, cut one piece of self fabric to the length of the strips and 2 inches deep. Cut a piece of lining to the same width and 6 inches deep.

26. Sew fabric to lining as shown and press seam down.

27. Sew fabric edge to top of upper strip and lining edge to bottom of lower strip, lifting the strips away from the coat to do so.

28. Smooth the lining down and machine stitch sides, lifting the ends of the strips as before.

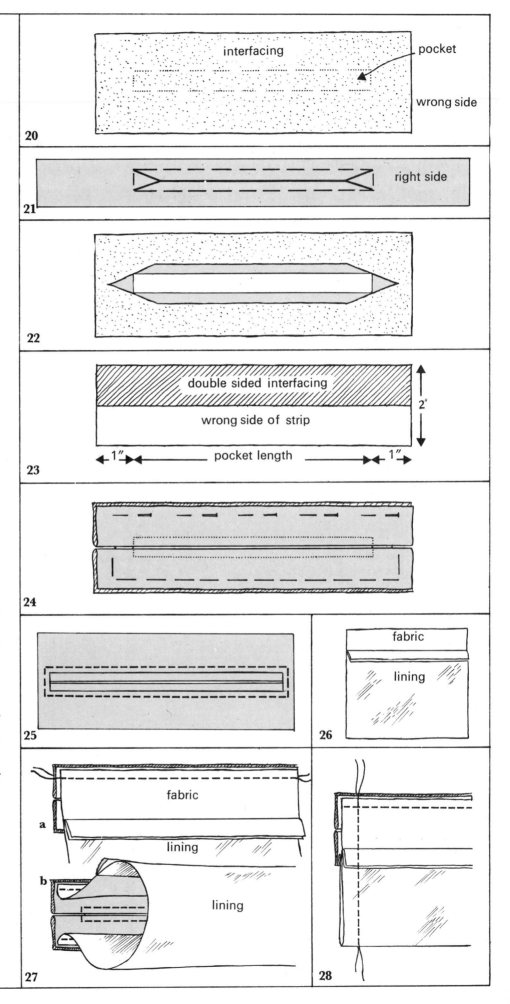

2280

Decorative pockets

Pockets are made using one of two basic methods. They can be made from self fabric which is applied to the garment, or they can be made of lining fabric pushed to the inside through a seam or slash opening. These pockets are sometimes covered by a welt or a flap. All the pocket designs given here are variations of these two basic constructions.

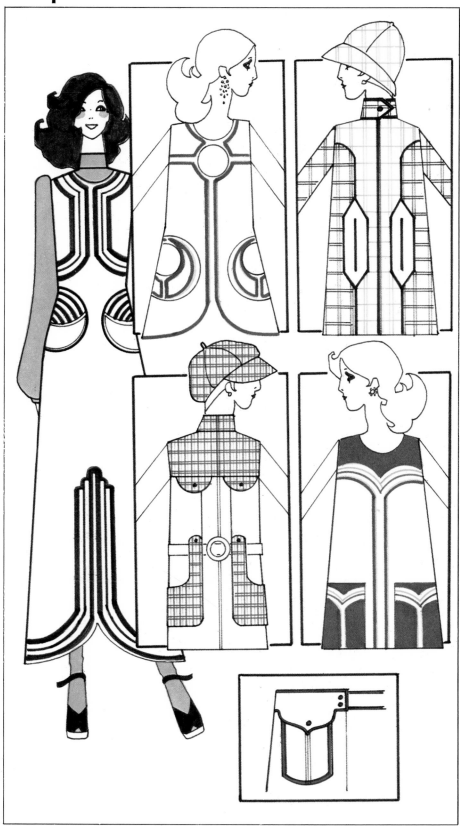

Preparation of pockets

To achieve a crisp and professional finish, it is essential to plan the preparation and the placing of the pockets carefully. The positioning of pockets is most important, as they are often the main styling feature of the garment. For pockets to be positioned below the waist, the main rule is that they should be placed at a level where the hands can be slipped into them naturally and comfortably. If they are placed too close to the hem they will look and feel awkward. In certain cases, however, the rules are flexible. Pockets above the waistline, and patch pockets placed anywhere, are usually strictly decorative so it is better to concentrate on whether the position is flattering, regardless of how inaccessible the pocket may be.

When making any pattern adjustments, do not overlook the pockets as they may require repositioning.

Interfacing pockets

All types of pockets made in loosely woven or lightweight fabrics need to be interfaced. The interfacing preserves the pocket line, provides added strength and reinforces the opening. A lightweight interfacing, placed on the underside of the garment, has sufficient body to give the finished pocket a crisp feel and appearance. Welts and flaps should also be interfaced to preserve their shape and resilience. The interfacing is usually cut on the bias grain to extend $\frac{5}{8}$ inch beyond the foldline. Patch pockets are not usually interfaced, but are generally lined for a good finish. To achieve accurate shaping when making patch pockets it is worth basting carefully around a paper template for both the shape of the pocket and the flap. This will insure that all the pockets on a garment are of the same size and shape. It also makes the machine stitching around curves much easier because it makes the fabric firmer. Any top-stitching lines should also be marked with basting stitches before the pocket is made. For top-stitching lines of an unusual shape such as in designs 12 and 16, make a separate template and mark the line with basting stitches.

The top-stitching should, whenever possible, be worked before the pocket is stitched to the garment.

Patch pockets

Patch pockets with a mock flap

Patch pockets can be made in virtually any shape desired and designs 1, 2, 3 and 4 are all based on a simple lined patch pocket with a mock flap. However, in

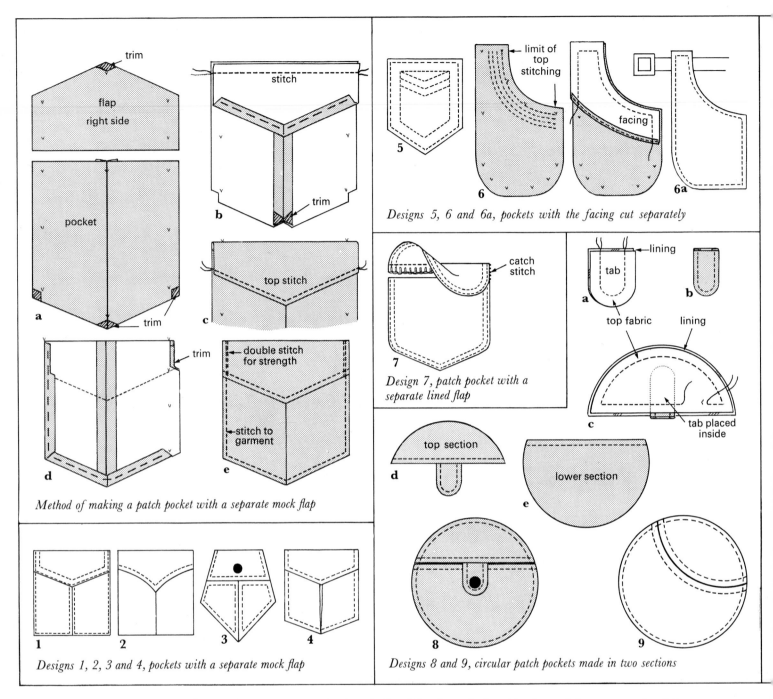

Method of making a patch pocket with a separate mock flap

Designs 5, 6 and 6a, pockets with the facing cut separately

Design 7, patch pocket with a separate lined flap

Designs 1, 2, 3 and 4, pockets with a separate mock flap

Designs 8 and 9, circular patch pockets made in two sections

the case of these pockets, the flap section is cut separately and turned over to the right side of the pocket, as they have either a seam or a pleat down the center.

Patch pockets with a separate facing

Designs 5, 6 and 6a are based on a simple lined patch pocket with the facing cut separately, which in this case is turned and hemmed to the wrong side of the pocket and not the right. The top-stitching on design 6 is worked before the facing is applied.

Design 6a is made in the same way as design 6. A space is left when the pocket is stitched to the garment through which a belt can be slotted.

Patch pocket with a separate flap

Design 7 is based on a simple, lined patch pocket but the lined flap is worked separately from the pocket and is fastened with a button and buttonhole. If the pocket is purely decorative then the button can be sewn on through all thicknesses of fabric, omitting the buttonhole.

Patch pockets based on circles

All these designs are based on the techniques of a simple, lined patch pocket. The opening of the pockets is either achieved by having a buttonhole type slit, two shapes made separately to form the circle, or a hole in the center of the circle.

Pockets made from two shapes

Designs 8 and 9 are constructed from two separate shapes, as shown.

Pocket with contrast backing

For design 10, the main pocket is made as a simple, lined patch but the top-stitched pocket backing is made separately (unlined) and extends into the pocket. The raw edge of the backing section is finished with buttonhole stitch worked through to the garment and it is covered by the main pocket overlapping it as shown.

Pockets with buttonhole slit opening

For designs 11 and 12, the pocket and lining are cut in two halves and seamed at either end of the straight edge, leaving an opening in the center to the required length. They are made up as shown. Alternatively, the same designs can be made by working a large bound buttonhole across a circular patch pocket.

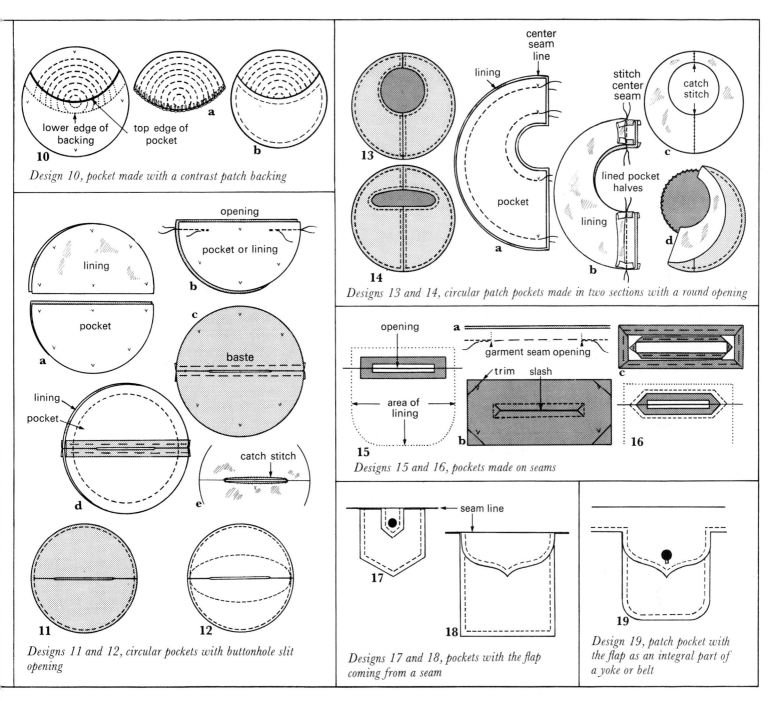

Design 10, pocket made with a contrast patch backing

10

13

14

Designs 13 and 14, circular patch pockets made in two sections with a round opening

a
b
c
d

11 **12**

Designs 11 and 12, circular pockets with buttonhole slit opening

15 **16**

Designs 15 and 16, pockets made on seams

17 **18**

Designs 17 and 18, pockets with the flap coming from a seam

19

Design 19, patch pocket with the flap as an integral part of a yoke or belt

On design 11, the inner line of top-stitching is marked around a template and worked first. The pocket is then top-stitched around the outer edge, directly onto the garment.

Pockets with a hole opening

Designs 13 and 14 are both based on two halves of a circle. A contrast backing is cut to a size larger than the intended circular opening and zigzag stitched in place directly onto the garment. The pocket is then placed centrally over the contrasting fabric and top-stitched in position.

Pockets in a seam

Seam pockets with a patch

Designs 15 and 16 are made in the same

way, using applied patches of different shapes over the seam as shown. Design 16 has a line of top-stitching worked the width of the machine foot away from the outer edge of the patch to give extra interest.

Cut a patch to the required shape and size, allowing $\frac{5}{8}$ inch turnings on the outer edges. Mark the size of the pocket opening on the patch and indicate the outer edge with basting stitches. Machine stay-stitch around the shape of the opening just inside the marked edge. Turn and baste all seam allowances to the back of the patch. Press carefully on the wrong side. Baste and slip-stitch the patch over the seam opening and press. Baste one piece of the lining fabric pocket to the wrong side of the opening and finish as for a bound buttonhole.

Lay the second lining piece onto the first and stitch all around the edge. Press and remove basting stitches from seam opening.

These pockets can be worked either into a seam across the garment or into a side seam. If the pocket is on a side seam, the pocket lining should be cut to the shape of a side pocket.

Flap or tab worked into seam

For designs 17 and 18, the main pocket is made as for a basic, lined patch pocket and the tab or flap is made separately and stitched into the seam of the garment, for example the yoke seam on a dress or jacket.

Design 19 is made in the same way except the flap is integral with a belt, waistband or a yoke.

2283

Decorative seams

Decorative seaming is a subtle way in which to add extra interest and individuality to a garment. Decorative seams are excellent for large or awkward figure shapes, for which a plain fabric is often more flattering. The plain fabric shows up the seams and reduces the overall impact of an ample figure. A small selection of decorated seams is shown on these pages but the variations are endless.

Here, a plain seam is decorated with top stitching worked with buttonhole twist wound onto the bobbin. Contrasting colors have been used for a bold effect.

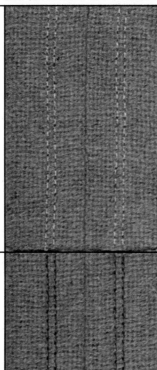

This plain seam is simply decorated with spaced lines of straight stitching in a self color. The stitching is worked using mercerized cotton thread, both on the bobbin and on top of the sewing machine, and the stitches made fairly long. Further lines of stitching could be added and the stitch adjusted to an even longer length if desired. However, too many lines of stitching would not look so attractive.

The top stitching here is worked as a zigzag stitch, the line closest to the seam being more widely spaced than the outer line.

A plain seam, decorated with spaced lines of straight stitching in a contrasting color. The contrasting color stands out and shows up better at a distance.

For more textural interest, the straight lines of top stitching have been worked here in wool which is wound onto the bobbin, and the zigzag lines with buttonhole twist wound onto the spool, with the bobbin case tension loosened. Mercerized thread is threaded on top of the machine with the tension set at normal. The thicker yarns should appear to be couched onto the fabric.

Several lines of straight stitching worked in different colors gives a softer effect.

Automatic patterns worked in a strong color contrast using mercerized thread, make pretty seam decorations. When using automatic patterns to form decorative top stitching, follow the instructions supplied with the sewing machine.

The automatic patterns can be combined with lines of satin stitch of varying widths or lines of straight stitching. Avoid working too many lines of stitching or the effect of the individual patterns will be lost.

This channel seam is dramatically heightened when backed with a strong contrasting color and top stitched with an automatic pattern in the same contrast.

This bound seam relies on color and textural contrast. Try using silk on wool; plain on patterned; bias weave (cut) and straight. Cut the bias binding strip approximately three times the width of the finished seam. With right sides together, stitch the binding along the stitch line on a single layer of fabric. Fold the binding over to the wrong side, baste and press. Place the inner edge of the binding on the right side of the seam line of the corresponding seam and work a line of stitching along the edge.

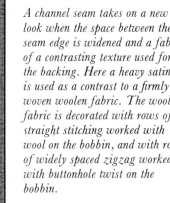

A channel seam takes on a new look when the space between the seam edge is widened and a fabric of a contrasting texture used for the backing. Here a heavy satin is used as a contrast to a firmly woven woolen fabric. The wool fabric is decorated with rows of straight stitching worked with wool on the bobbin, and with rows of widely spaced zigzag worked with buttonhole twist on the bobbin.

A piped seam can be successfully used for curved seams as the piping fabric is cut on the bias grain of the fabric. The piping can be of piping cord, quilting wool, chunky knitting wool or similar yarns.
If the piping cord is bulky, when joining a seam, cut it off even with the stitching line, leaving the binding fabric to continue under the seam. This is necessary to reduce bulk.

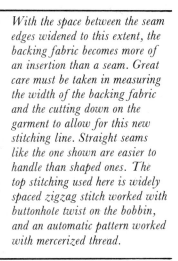

With the space between the seam edges widened to this extent, the backing fabric becomes more of an insertion than a seam. Great care must be taken in measuring the width of the backing fabric and the cutting down on the garment to allow for this new stitching line. Straight seams like the one shown are easier to handle than shaped ones. The top stitching used here is widely spaced zigzag stitch worked with buttonhole twist on the bobbin, and an automatic pattern worked with mercerized thread.

If the piping is narrow, some additional straight top stitching can be incorporated as extra decoration.
As this seam faces in one direction, the piping must be stitched to the top layer of the garment first to insure a good line and then a second line of stitching next to the first, worked to join the seam.

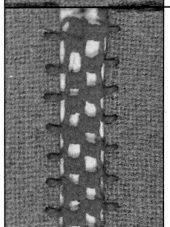

Insertions make very pretty seam decorations. Here, Italian buttonhole insertion stitch has been worked in buttonhole twist in a bright contrasting color for a striking effect. There are many insertion stitches to choose from, some of which form a stronger joining medium than others. The stitch and the type of yarn should be carefully chosen according to the type of fabric to be worked on. Heavy-weight insertions, for example, are not suitable for fine, delicate fabrics.

ADVANCED DRESSMAKING

Quick ways in sewing

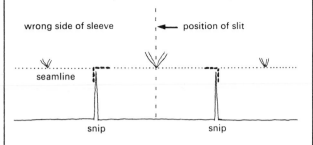

1. *Alternative cuff opening*

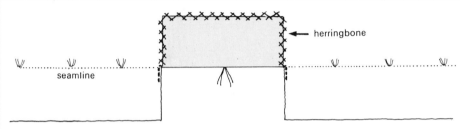

2. *The marked opening*

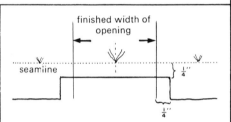

3. *The herringboned opening*

For the dressmaker who prefers to substitute some of her own methods when making up a commercial pattern, here are some useful tips. There is a couture hint for a perfect finish – covering snap fasteners and hooks and eyes – a quick way of finishing a cuffed sleeve and opening, and an easy way of putting in sleeves.

Cuff openings

1. If you wish to avoid making the usual slit openings, here is a good alternative which is quicker and easier to work. The opening edge can be finished in two ways, the choice of finish being determined by the thickness of the fabric used.

Thick fabrics
This finish is for heavier fabrics, such as linen and wool, only.
2. Before removing the pattern piece from the fabric, make a tailor's tack at the bottom of the marked slit position on the pattern. Decide on the finished width of the opening – usually 1 to 1½ inches – and mark it centrally on the tailor's tack as shown (figure 2).
Strengthen the corners with stay stitching, then snip up to the sewing line.
3. Fold the cut piece to the wrong side and herringbone in place.
Stitch on the cuff as shown in **1** to finish.

Thin fabrics
This finish is particularly good for fine cottons and sheer fabrics.

4. Before removing the pattern pieces from the fabric, make a tailor's tack at the bottom of the marked slit position on the pattern. Decide on the finished width of the opening – usually 1 to 1½ inches – and mark it centrally over the tailor's tack as shown. Then trim the seam allowance along the opening to ¼ inch and extend the trimming ¼ inch past the opening on each side.
5. Working on the wrong side, turn up a narrow rolled hem. The hem will be slightly longer than the finished opening so that the cuff will cover the ends and there will not be any weak corners.

Shirt cuff

Here is a good way to make an interfaced cuff with a neat, flat wrist edge which can easily be substituted for any method given in a pattern's instructions. This cuff is made from one piece of fabric folded over at the wrist edge, so for each cuff you will need a piece of fabric double the cuff depth. If your cuff pattern has a seam at the wrist, simply eliminate the seam by placing the wrist stitching line to a fabric fold.
6. Cut a piece of interfacing to the cuff length and ½ inch deeper than the folded cuff depth.
Position the interfacing to the wrong side of the cuff as shown and machine stitch to the cuff just inside the inner edge of the interfacing.
Fold the cuff along the fold line, right sides facing, and make in the usual way with the interfaced half placed to the top of the cuff. The stitching line will fall to the underneath out of sight.

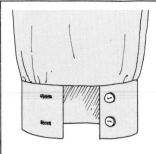

4. *The trimmed seam allowance*

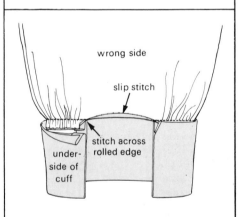

5. *Cuff stitched in place from the wrong side*

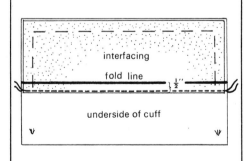

6. *The interfacing positioned on cuff*

Sleeves

If you have difficulty in sewing in sleeves here is an alternative method which is especially good on children's clothes where the sleeve head is small. This method is often used on mass-produced clothes.

After fitting the garment, unbaste the side and sleeve seams.

Stitch, make neat and press the shoulder seams.

7. Match the correct sleeve to its armhole with the right sides facing, and pin all matching balance points. Smooth down the ease with your finger tips and pin.

Baste and then stitch as shown, leaving about 1 inch unstitched at each side of the underarm.

Stitch the side seam and the sleeve seam. Make the seam allowances neat and press them open.

8. Complete the underarm seam as shown.

A couture touch

A really special garment in an expensive fabric deserves a couture finish. If you are using snap fasteners or hooks and eyes on the garment, follow the couturier by covering them.

Covering a snap fastener

9 a, b, c. To cover a snap fastener cut two circles of fabric as shown (**a**). The fabric for covering should be fine, so it may be necessary to use a matching lining fabric.

Work a gathering stitch around the outer edge of each.

Cover each half of the fastener by drawing up the fabric to the wrong side of it and, in the case of the ball section, piercing the ball through the center of the fabric (**b**).

Finish off the thread at the back and stitch the snap fastener on (**c**).

Covering hooks and eyes

10. Using matching double thread, cover the hooks and eyes with buttonhole stitch as shown. This way they will blend in with the garment and be inconspicuous.

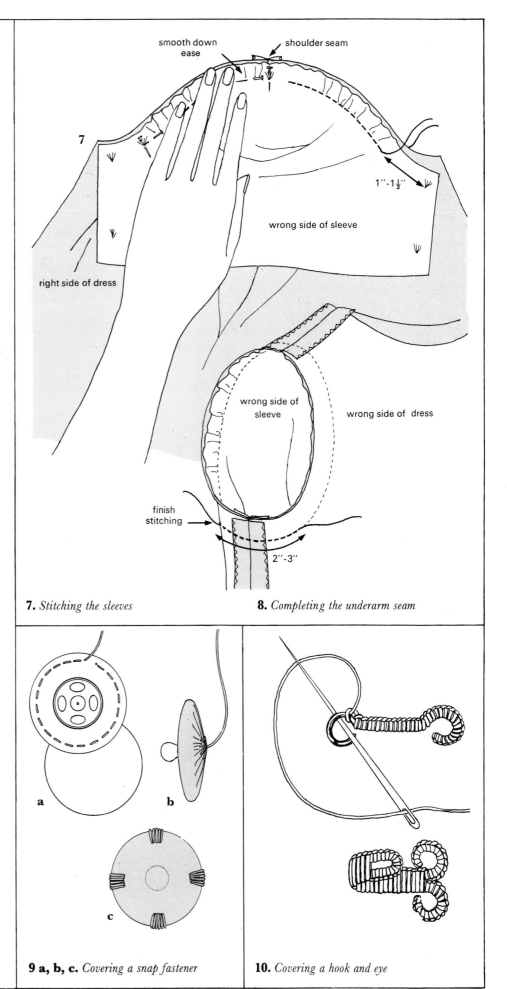

7. Stitching the sleeves

8. Completing the underarm seam

9 a, b, c. Covering a snap fastener

10. Covering a hook and eye

ADVANCED DRESSMAKING

Interfacings

Interfacing is used to strengthen, to give a good shape to a garment and to prevent stretching. It adds body and crispness to areas such as collars, cuffs, necklines, belts and behind buttons. Interfacing can also be used to add firmness and roundness to the hems of skirts and sleeves made from medium or heavier-weight fabrics. There is a wide selection of interfacings to choose from, each suited to a certain process or type of fabric. Interfacings may be made especially or may be fabrics like organdy or net.

General usage

First decide how crisp you want the interfaced areas to be and whether some areas require more body than others. Collars and pocket flaps, for instance, may look better with a slightly heavier interfacing than for areas such as front facings or hem lines. In general, it is advisable to choose an interfacing which is of the same weight or slightly lighter than the fabric being worked. Never use one that is thicker, because the interfacing should blend into the garment,

doing its job without being noticeable. If in doubt, use a slightly lighter weight interfacing.

If a soft effect is desired, place the edge of the interfacing into the folded edge of the top fabric. If the fabric falls over the interfacing in a soft roll, it is the correct interfacing to use. If sharp points and a hard edge are formed, it is the wrong one.

Another general rule is to match the fiber content of the interfacing to that of the fabric. For example, choose a silk interfacing such as organza for silk, and canvas for a woolen fabric.

Unless using an iron-on or non-woven type, the interfacing should be ironed before it is cut out. If a garment is washable, the interfacing should be washable too and must be pre-shrunk before use.

Types of interfacing

Interfacings can be divided into three main groups – woven, non-woven and iron-on.

Non-woven interfacings

This type of interfacing is manufactured in a variety of weights and is available in either black, white, or gray, 25 inches and 37 inches wide. It comes in regular and all-bias types.

Non-woven interfacings are best used where a stand-up, sculptured effect is required. These interfacings are tested and designed for use with special fabrics and usually carry the manufacturer's recommendations for use and combinations with fabrics. However, it is always

advisable to test a piece on a scrap of the top fabric before using it on the garment. They are rarely suitable for use with sheer or semi-transparent fabrics, as they show through.

Iron-on non-woven interfacing

Iron-on non-woven interfacings are available in the same width and colors as the non-woven interfacings but not in such a variety of weights. They are useful for belts, pocket flaps and cuffs but great care must be taken when applying them, or the interfacing will "bubble" and spoil the finished look of the garment. Lay the fabric piece (usually the facing) right side down on the ironing board and place the interfacing on this with the adhesive side facing downward. Cover with a damp cloth and hold a medium hot iron over the cloth for 15 seconds. Lift the iron away and repeat the process until the whole surface has been ironed. The interfacing should now be fused to the fabric (figure 4). Unfortunately, once they are ironed on these interfacings do not always stay permanently in place and sometimes work loose unless they are held in position with a row of stitching around the edges.

Iron-on non-woven interfacings are not suitable for covering large areas, nor are they suitable for garments which receive frequent laundering as they will part from the fabric and cause "bubbling". Always test iron-on interfacings first on a spare piece of fabric in case the adhesive shows through.

Non-woven and iron-on interfacings should never be used on silks, or sheer fabrics.

Iron-on woven interfacings

This type of interfacing is made from a finely woven cotton with an adhesive backing. It has, to a certain extent, the same disadvantages as the non-woven iron-on interfacings but it is more pliable and blends better with the fabric. It can be used with cotton, linen, medium and heavy-weight rayons of the linen weave type. It can also be used quite successfully on certain fine cotton fabrics, but it is essential to test a piece on a scrap of the top fabric before using it on the garment. This type of interfacing is generally best ironed onto the facing fabric rather than the top fabric. The edges can then be held by the seam and the loose edge finished with the top fabric to hold it securely in position. This type of interfacing is most useful for stiffening blouse and shirt collars and cuffs because several layers (up to three or four) can be ironed on to achieve the required stiffness. These layers should be ironed onto the under collar and sleeve facings, and the interfacing should

Outside fabric	correct interfacing
Dress weight: cotton linen wool	pre-shrunk treated lawn iron-on or non-woven interfacing as recommended by the manufacturer
Suit-weight: cotton linen wool	treated cotton interfacing, such as bleached muslin iron-on or non-woven interfacing as recommended by the manufacturer
Man-made fiber fabrics	non-woven interfacing as recommended by the manufacturer for very light fabrics (lawn, voile, etc.) pure silk or nylon organza
Pure silk	fine lawn or pure silk organza
See-through fabrics	soft organdy or pure silk organza

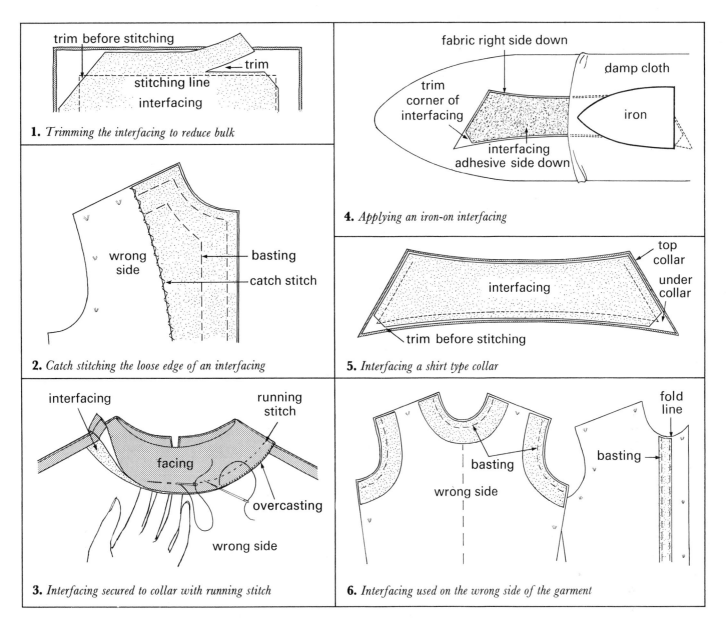

1. *Trimming the interfacing to reduce bulk*

2. *Catch stitching the loose edge of an interfacing*

3. *Interfacing secured to collar with running stitch*

4. *Applying an iron-on interfacing*

5. *Interfacing a shirt type collar*

6. *Interfacing used on the wrong side of the garment*

be cut just a fraction beyond the stitching line so that it can be caught in the seam. It is not possible to trim the interfacing back after stitching because it is usually stuck so firmly to the fabric.

Woven canvas interfacings

Woven interfacings are made in the same way as woven fabrics with lengthwise and crosswise threads, i.e. with a grain, They should therefore be cut on the same grain as the top fabric to which the piece is to be applied.

Woven interfacings are made from different types of canvas such as hair canvas, cotton canvas, linen canvas and a variety of finer weaves in varying degrees of stiffness. It is advisable to shrink these interfacings before use by pressing them well under a damp cloth. Woven canvas interfacings are suitable for woolen fabrics and tailoring weight linens.

Other woven interfacings

Cotton organdy, silk or nylon organza, lawn and cotton or nylon net are the types of interfacing best suited to use with light-weight fabrics such as fine cotton, silks, sheer and semi-transparent fabrics.

Interfacings in dressmaking

Mark the pieces of interfacing with the same construction symbols as found on the pattern for easy matching with the top fabric. Darts should be marked on both the interfacing and the top fabric as they are stitched separately.

The interfacings are sewn into the seams when the garment is being made up, and trimmed back to the machine line to avoid bulky seams. To avoid excess bulk at the sharp corners on collars and cuffs, trim the corners off about $\frac{1}{4}$ inch inside the meeting point of the seam before stitching the interfacing in place (figure 1).

Where one edge of the interfacing is not sewn into a seam it can either be left free, sewn onto the garment with catch stitching, figure 2 (not suitable for fine fabrics as the stitches show through), or sewn onto the facing with tiny running stitches after the facing has been sewn to the garment and turned to the wrong side (figure 3).

When interfacing roll and shirt type collars, the interfacing is placed on the undercollar (figure 5).

For plain necklines, sleeveless armholes, behind buttonholes and buttons, the interfacing is placed to the wrong side of the garment (figure 6), not to the facing. The raw edges of the facings are caught onto the top fabric with a catch stitch. (Iron-on and non-woven interfacings are not suitable for this technique).

For cuffs and stand-up collars the interfacing is placed to the wrong side of the top fabric. If a crisp effect is required, place the interfacing on the outer collar or cuff, and for a softer effect on the under collar or cuff facing.

ADVANCED DRESSMAKING

Working with pleats

Pleats are folds of fabric which provide controlled fullness in certain parts of a garment. They can be placed either singly or in a series, and can be pressed flat or left unpressed, as the style of the garment dictates. Pressed pleats give a smooth, slimming line to a garment and unpressed pleats a softer, fuller shape.

Fabrics

The type of fabric dictates how the pleats hang, so choose it carefully. Consider the grain and check the layout given with the pattern, remembering that pleats on the lengthwise grain fall well, while those on the crosswise grain tend to bunch out.

Any firmly woven fabric such as wool, gabardine or linen will hold a pleat well, but pleats in loosely woven fabrics, knits and silk look better if they are top-stitched.

Patterns for pleated skirts should be bought by the hip measurement and patterns with pleated bodices by the bust measurement.

If any alteration in width is required, distribute it evenly throughout all the pleats to keep them uniform. When tapering pleats to fit the waistline, keep the top fold on the same grain and make any adjustment to the under fold, remembering to distribute alterations evenly.

Types of pleat

Box pleats. These are made by making two equal folds and turning them away from each other, the under folds meeting in the center beneath the pleat (Fig. 1).

Inverted pleats. Inverted pleats are the reverse of box pleats. Two folds of equal depth are turned toward each other to meet at the center, the fullness lying underneath (Fig. 2).

Knife pleats. These are narrow folds all running in the same direction. For comfort, ease of movement and correct hang, knife pleats are sometimes cut $\frac{1}{2}$ to $\frac{3}{4}$ inch wider at the hem (Fig. 3).

Straight pleats. These pleats are the same width for their full length. They can be folded over each other to fit into a waistband, or used as a decorative panel on a skirt or dress.

Unpressed pleats. Unpressed pleats can be folded in the same way as pressed pleats, but are left to hang free and take their own line.

If a bunchy effect is required for a particular design, the fabric should be cut on the crosswise grain. For example, a full-headed two-piece sleeve looks better if the top part is cut in this way (Fig. 4).

A bunchy effect is not generally suitable for unpressed pleats on a skirt, so cut on the lengthwise grain of the fabric. Never try to save material by cutting one skirt pattern piece on the lengthwise grain and the other on the crosswise grain of the fabric – the effect can be disastrous.

Contrasting fabric inverted pleat. Inverted pleat underlays can look attractive in a contrasting material. If the pattern does not have a separate piece for the underlay, adjust it as follows. Cut the pattern on the under fold line and add $\frac{5}{8}$ inch turning to all cut edges.

Sew the contrasting fabric to the under fold line before making the pleat (Fig. 5).

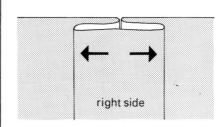

1. *Box pleat*

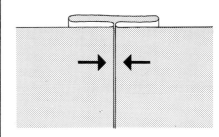

2. *Inverted pleat*

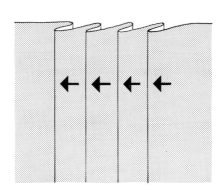

3. *Knife pleats*

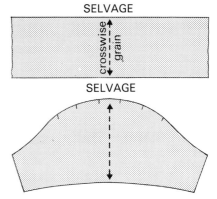

4. *Cut sleeve top on crosswise grain*

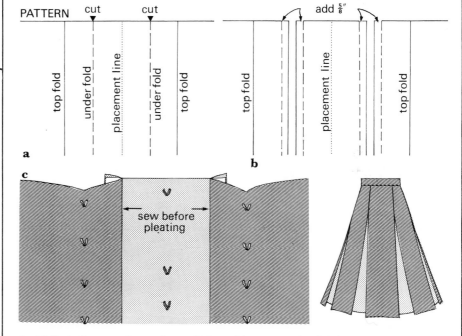

5. *Method of constructing an inverted pleat with a contrasting fabric*

Top-stitching pleats

It is possible to make a fashion feature of top-stitched pleats. Baste the pleats flat through all the layers of fabric before stitching. A bold effect is required, so use a large needle in the sewing machine, set the machine to the longest stitch and use buttonhole twist for both threads.

Before working the top-stitching on a garment, take a spare piece of the fabric, make some pleats and practice the stitches, adjusting the tension until the desired effect is achieved.

Fine fabrics which do not hold a pleat well are best top-stitched along both top and under folds for the entire length of the pleat.

As long as the pleat is on the straight grain of the fabric, it can be stitched either from the top or the bottom. If the grain is not straight it is better to stitch from the bottom of the pleat upward to avoid stretching the fabric (Fig. 6).

If the fabric is stretched it will create a slight fullness at the hem which means that the pleat will not hang straight.

The best stage at which to work the top-stitching is before the skirt is sewn onto the waistband or the bodice, and after the hemline is finished.

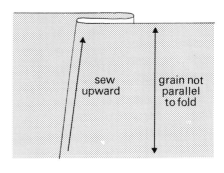

6. *Directions in which to stitch pleats*

The general construction of pleats

All pleats should be shaped with precision, so always transfer the pattern markings accurately, using different colored tailor tacks for the top and under folds and for the placement line (Fig. 7). Lay the fabric on a flat surface. An ironing board is ideal, as the fabric can be pinned to the cover when the initial folding takes place. Pin each pleat at the upper and lower ends and then along the length, keeping it free from the under layer (Fig. 8).

Beginning at the lower edge, baste the pleat folds on the right side, then turn the fabric over and baste the folds on the wrong side. Baste down any which are to be top-stitched. Baste across pleats at waistline and baste the whole garment for fitting (Fig. 9).

Fitting

When the skirt is basted, try it on to make sure that the pleats hang straight. If the skirt is tight over the hips or stomach, adjust each pleat under fold until it hangs correctly. However, the problem should not arise if the pattern has been adjusted correctly before cutting out.

If the pleats spring open at the hem, raise the waistline. Pin the skirt to a length of tape fastened around the waist, and raise the tape until the pleats hang straight. Adjust the under folds evenly.

If the pleats overlap at the hem, lower the waist slightly in the same way and adjust the pleat under folds evenly.

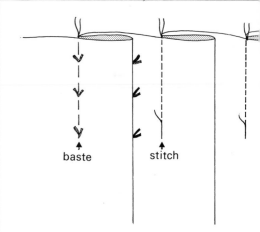

10. *Stitch knife pleats on the wrong side*

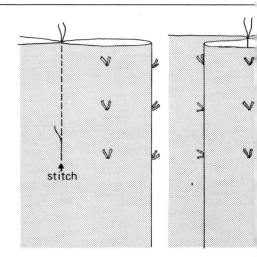

11. *Stitch box pleats on the right side*

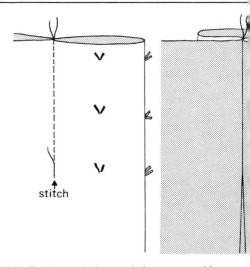

12. *For inverted pleats, stitch on wrong side*

Finishing the pleats

When finishing pleats always work with the front and back of the skirt separated. Mark any fitting alterations before unbasting the side seams and starting work on the pleats.

Top-stitch knife pleats on the wrong side for a smooth effect, making sure to finish them securely at the lower end

7. *Mark all fold lines accurately*

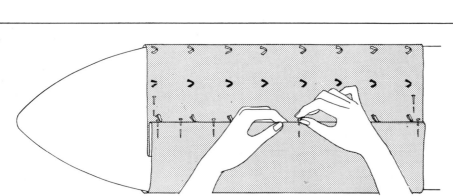

8. *Pin each pleat at lower and upper ends and then along the length*

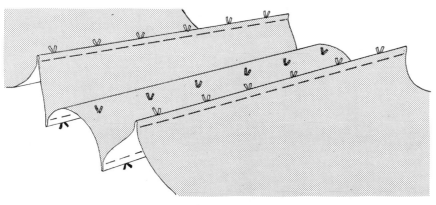

9. *Baste the pleat folds on the right side, then baste those on the wrong side*

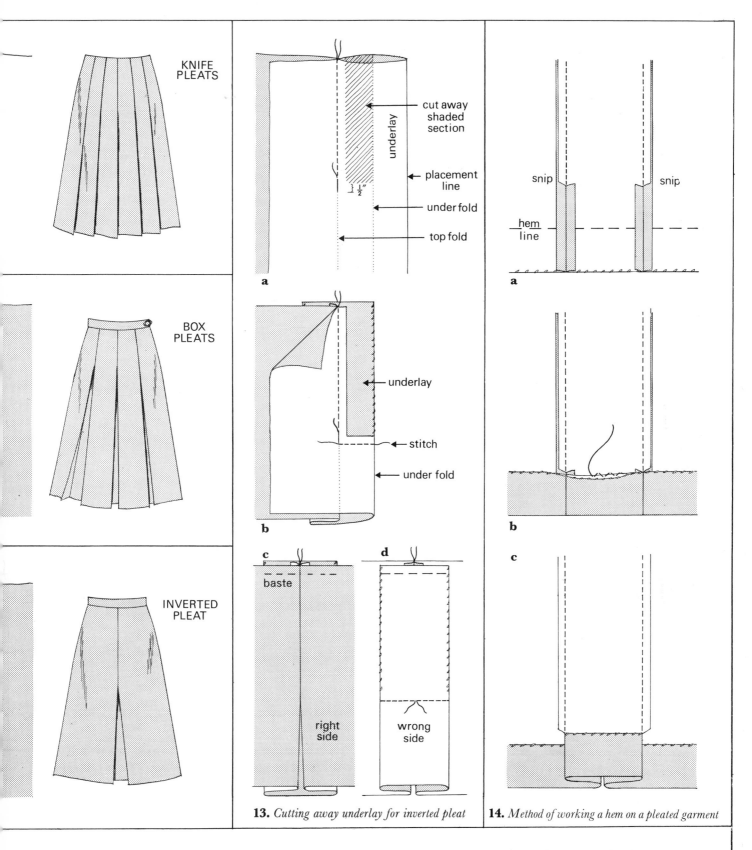

KNIFE PLEATS

BOX PLEATS

INVERTED PLEAT

cut away shaded section

underlay

placement line

$\frac{1}{2}''$

under fold

top fold

a

underlay

stitch

under fold

b

baste

c

right side

d

wrong side

13. *Cutting away underlay for inverted pleat*

snip

snip

hem line

a

b

c

14. *Method of working a hem on a pleated garment*

(Fig. 10).
Stitch box pleats on the right side for desired length and press pleat flat. (Fig. 11). Stitch inverted pleats on the wrong side and press flat (Fig. 12). If inverted pleats are being made in a heavy material, a section of the under fold can be cut away as shown, to reduce bulk (Figs. 13a–d).
Machine stitch pleat to the length required and cut away half the under pleat as shown. Make the outside raw edge neat and machine stitch across each side of the pleat, keeping the fold away from the background fabric. Baste across the top of the pleat.

Hemming pleated skirts
Run a line of basting stitches along the hem line. Trim the hem evenly and overcast the raw edge. Measure the hem depth above the hemline and snip seams at this point. Press the seam flat above the snip and open below it (Fig. 14). Slip stitch hem, rebaste pleats and press.

ADVANCED DRESSMAKING
Lining a coat or a jacket

The lining in a tailored coat or jacket combines several important functions. It covers the internal canvassing and seams, prolongs the life of the coat and makes it much easier to wear, slipping easily over sweaters and dresses.

When a coat outlasts its lining it is possible to re-line it, using the original lining as a pattern. The treatment of the hem is the only difference between lining a coat and a jacket. A coat lining is usually left free, whereas a jacket lining is stitched down.

Lining fabric

There are many lining fabrics to choose from, all of which will give the required "silky" finish to the coat; but do not be tempted to buy the cheapest types as these tend to split in wear. Always consider the weight of the coat fabric before making a final choice.

For heavy weight coats
Use synthetics with a satin weave. For extra warmth use Milium, which has a satin weave face and is backed with a fine layer of aluminum.

For medium weight coats
Use synthetics with a plain weave.

For light weight coats
Use synthetic taffeta.
For a very special coat use a pure silk lining. This is expensive, but it gives a really luxurious finish. Avoid using crepe lining as this will stretch in wear and become very uncomfortable.

Lining a coat or jacket

The pattern
When lining a new coat or jacket, use the lining pieces given with the pattern and cut them out according to the layout instructions.

To re-line an old coat or jacket, take out the lining carefully, rip the seams and darts or pleats and iron the pieces flat. Using these pieces as patterns, lay them on the new lining fabric,

matching the grains exactly (Fig. 1).

Making the lining
Before starting to make the lining, test iron a spare piece of the fabric to find the temperature needed to make a good flat seam without melting the fibers. This temperature can be quite critical, so if the iron has been on for some time, re-test it before ironing the new lining. Start by pinning, basting, stitching and ironing the darts and/or pleats. Then stitch all the seams except the shoulder and armholes (Fig. 2).

Most lining fabrics fray quickly when cut, so make neat the seam allowances by turning under $\frac{1}{8}$ inch and top-stitching (Fig. 3).

A new coat should be finished and pressed and an old coat should be cleaned professionally, or brushed and pressed, before the lining is sewn in.

Pinning in the lining
If you have a dressmaker's dummy, put the coat onto it, wrong side out, turning the sleeves flat to the inside. Fasten the coat buttons and adjust it so that the seams are vertical and the hem line is straight (Fig. 4).

If a dummy is not available, lay the coat right side down on a table or an ironing board and work each section as flat as possible.

Take the lining and place it to the coat, wrong sides together. The lining pieces

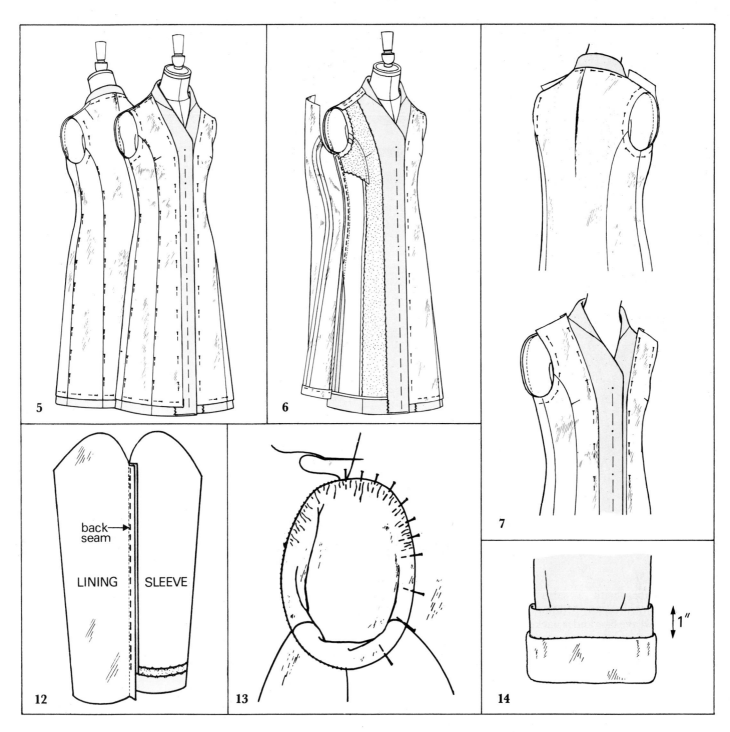

are first pinned together, so work in the following order.

Seams
Pin down from top to bottom of any style seams at the back, the side seams, the fronts from the center back point and the center pleat (if there is one).

Armhole
The canvassing should have held the armhole shape, but if there has been any stretching during the making do not cut the lining to match. Instead, ease the coat to the lining, to regain the original line.

Then pin along the shoulder seams, overlapping the front over the back.

Hem
For a coat, pin the lining up 1 inch above the coat hem.

For a jacket, pin the lining hem the exact length of the jacket hem.

At this stage it is a good idea to slip the coat or jacket on to see if the lining is pulling at any point (Fig. 5).

Stitching the coat lining
The lining must be attached firmly inside the coat or jacket to prevent it from moving in wear, so lift the lining and baste the side seams of the coat and lining together from the underarm to the hip level, unpinning where necessary. (Fig. 6).

Next, turn under the seam allowances along the neck, front edges and front shoulders and re-pin in smooth lines (Fig. 7). Even the hem to leave a $1\frac{1}{2}$ inch to 2 inch turning. Turn under $\frac{1}{2}$ inch and baste. Stitch the lining to the coat with felling stitch for a really professional finish (Fig. 8.).

Hem. Press the hem before sewing in the rest of the lining.

Shoulder seams. Check that the front seam allowance laps over the back (Fig. 9).

Outer edge. Work each side from the center back to the hem line to avoid any movement of the lining as you sew (Fig. 10).

Armhole. Working from the inside of the sleeves, sew the lining to the coat

2295

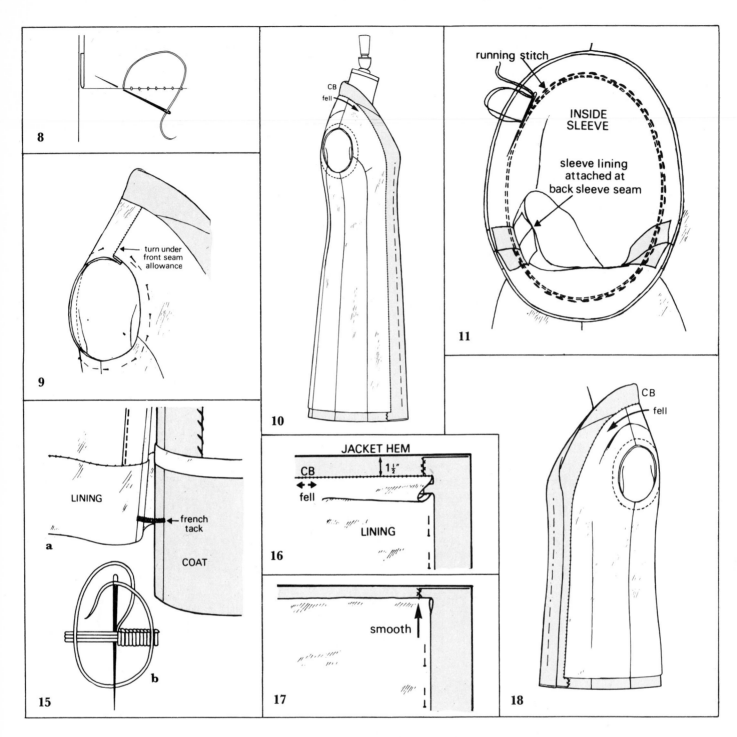

$\frac{1}{8}$ inch to $\frac{1}{4}$ inch outside the coat stitching line. This stitching must be very firm, so use a double thread and a small running stitch (Fig. 11).

Stitching the sleeve lining

To avoid movement in wear, the sleeve lining is sewn into the sleeve in the same way as the coat lining is sewn to the coat.

Turn the coat sleeve through to the wrong side and place the wrong side of the lining to the sleeve, matching the underarm seams, or the back seams with a two-piece sleeve. Baste together (Fig. 12).

Turn the sleeve back to the right side, taking the lining with it.

At the sleeve head, bring the sleeve lining up, turn under the seam allowance and pin to cover the small running stitches. Adjust the lining sleeve head fullness into tiny pleats and fell firmly (Fig. 13).

At the sleeve hem, turn under the lining hem $\frac{5}{8}$ inch and fell 1 inch above the sleeve hem line (Fig. 14).

French tacks

To hold a lining at the hem, make French tacks between the lining and coat side seams (Fig. 15).

Stitching a jacket lining

Pin the lining into the jacket as described under "Pinning in the lining" and

try the jacket on to check that the lining is not pulling.

At the hem, lift the lining fold 1 inch to $1\frac{1}{2}$ inches above the jacket edge and turn the front seam allowances to the wrong side. Fell firmly (Fig. 16).

Continue as for the coat until the shoulders and armholes have been stitched, and the outer edges turned under and pinned, smoothing the front lining down into a fold at the hem edge (Fig. 17).

Fell from the center back as for the coat (Fig. 18).

The extra length in the lining provided by the fold at the hem allows for ease of movement when the jacket is worn. Fell the sleeve lining as for the coat.

ADVANCED DRESSMAKING

Tailoring techniques

Tailoring demands a certain amount of time and effort, as well as a knowledge of special techniques. The methods dealt with here include molding and shaping by pressing and with the aid of supporting canvases, plus the special stitches used in sewing.

Canvasing the coat

Two groups of canvases or interfacings are used in tailoring. Both groups are made up of woven fibers so that the grain lines of the main fabric and the interfacing can be exactly matched.

Mixed fiber hair canvases

Wool and hair. A smooth, grayish fabric which is very springy and does not crease. It keeps the shapes molded into it better than any other canvas.

Cotton and hair. This type of canvas is slightly springy, but it can crease.

Single fiber interfacings

Pure wool. A smooth, creamy-colored fabric which is very springy and soft. It is useful for lightweight tweeds and also for completely interlining a garment where extra warmth is needed.

Linen canvas (or shrunk duck). A soft canvas which will maintain a crease. It is used with lightweight fabrics or linens and as a backing for pockets and hems.

French canvas (or collar canvas). This canvas is made with the warp and weft threads of equal weight to give firm control to the undercollar.

Shrinking

Canvases should always be pre-shrunk before use, either by wrapping in a damp sheet overnight and ironing the next day, or by pressing all over with a hot iron and a wet cloth and leaving to dry.
Linen stay tape $\frac{1}{2}$ inch wide should also be pre-shrunk by washing and ironing dry.

Canvas pattern pieces

Use the appropriate pieces given with the pattern, or cut your own from the front and back pieces.
For each front cut one piece of canvas as for the facing, adding an extra 1 inch seam allowance at the inner edge (Fig. 1), or if the pattern has a side front seam, use the front pattern complete instead of the facing pattern (Fig. 2).
Cut a second piece of interfacing for each front to include the armhole as shown, using the front or side front piece as a guide (Figs. 3a and b).
For the back, cut the canvas to include the neck and armhole using the back pattern as a guide, and curving the lower edge as shown (Fig. 4a).
If there is a center back seam, cut two

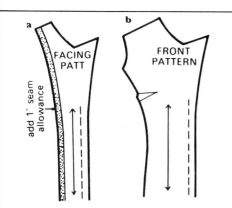

Center front interfacing: **1.** *using facing pattern*
2. *Using front pattern*

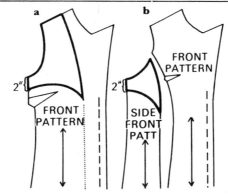

3. *Side front interfacing:* **a.** *for front without side front seams;* **b.** *for front with side front seam*

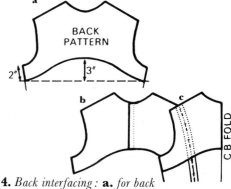

4. *Back interfacing:* **a.** *for back without seams;* **b.** *for back with center back seams;* **c.** *for back with side back seams*

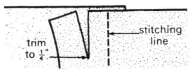

8. *Stitching interfacing seams*

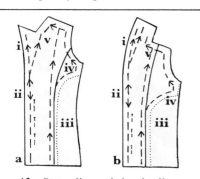

9a *and* **b.** *Step collar and shawl collar*

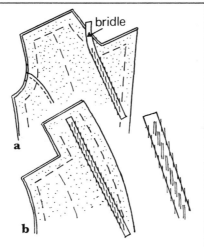

10a *and* **b.** *Pad stitch the stay tape to the crease line*

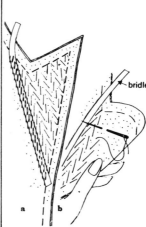

11a *and* **b.** *Pad stitching the step collar*

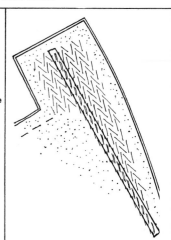

12. *For a shawl collar, pad stitch between the crease line and the neck edge*

pieces and join by overlapping on the seam line (Fig. 4b).

Where there are side back seams, overlap the pattern pieces on the stitching line (Fig. 4c). Always keep to the pattern grain lines.

Before any machine stitching is attempted, the coat shell must be basted together, the canvas basted into the shell with the grain lines matching, and the coat must be tried on for fit (Fig. 5).

Mark where the lapel crease lines fall (Fig. 6).

Shaping the canvas
Darts. Cut out the dart shape along the stitching line, place the cut edges over stay tape and machine stitch (Fig. 7).

Seams. Overlay the seams on the stitching lines and stitch. Trim the seam allowance back to $\frac{1}{4}$ inch (Fig. 8). Press over a tailor's ham to retain the shapes thus created.

Canvasing the front and back
The canvas is sewn in place after any style seams, darts and back seams have been stitched and pressed, but before the shoulder and side seams are stitched.

Front. Lay the interfacing flat on the table, over it lay the corresponding coat front, with the wrong side of the coat fabric toward the canvas (Figs. 9a and b). Match and pin the center and crease lines together (Fig. 9i).

Working from the bust line upward, baste the front edge to the canvas, smoothing it to prevent wrinkles (Fig. 9 ii). Repeat from the bust line downward (Fig. 9 iii).

Baste the opposite edge of the canvas from hem to shoulder (Fig. 9 iv).

Finally baste around armhole, shoulder, neck and along the crease line (Fig. 9 v).

A bridle. This is a length of stay tape used to support the crease line. This goes right along the crease line for a shawl collar, and 2 inches beyond for a step collar.

Pin the stay tape centrally along the crease line, keeping it taut. Using a double matching silk thread, pad stitch the stay tape centrally in place. Pad stitch each edge with single thread (Figs. 10a and b).

Remove the collar or lapel edge basting and continue to work rows of staggered pad stitching, keeping the rows in line with the bridle. Roll the work over the hand to help create the "roll" which will enable the collar or lapel to lie correctly (Figs. 11a and b).

For a shawl collar, pad stitch between the crease line and the neck edge (Fig. 12).

Another length of stay tape is sewed to the front seam edge to retain its shape.

Trim the front edge of the canvas just within the sewing line of the coat to reduce bulk in the seam. Cut the stay tape to the required length and center it over the sewing line (Figs. 13a, b and c). Baste the tape firmly along the outside edge and catch stitch the inner edge to the canvas (Fig. 14).

To finish attaching the canvas to the coat, trim the shoulder and underarm seams to just within the sewing line of the coat. Catch stitch down carefully (Figs. 15a and b).

To press the lapel, steam it firmly over the pad stitching and roll it on the crease line – do not press it flat.

Back. Lay the canvas to the wrong side of the coat and baste. Trim the shoulder

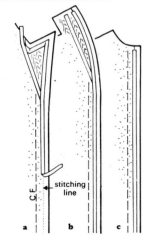

5. *Preparing for first fitting:* **a.** *back;* **b.** *front;* **c.** *under collar;* **d.** *overbasting shoulder side and neck seams*

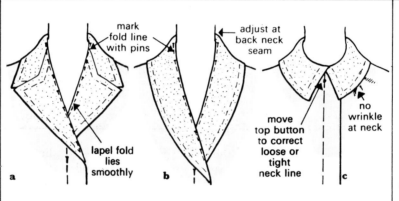

6. *Fitting a collar:* **a.** *step collar;* **b.** *shawl collar;* **c.** *coat without lapels*

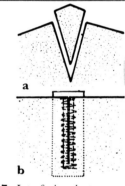

7. *Interfacing darts:* **a.** *cutting out dart;* **b.** *stitching dart together on stay tape*

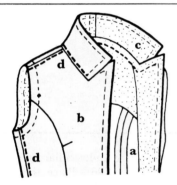

13. *Stay tape stitched to front of coat with:* **a.** *step collar;* **b.** *shawl collar;* **c.** *coat without lapels*

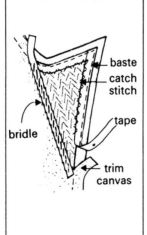

14. *Sewing on stay tape*

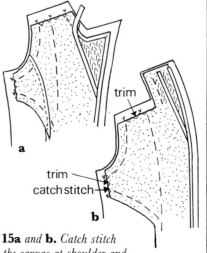

15a *and* **b.** *Catch stitch the canvas at shoulder and underarm seams on front*

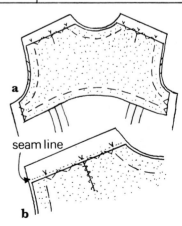

16a *and* **b.** *Catch stitch the canvas at shoulder and underarm seams on back*

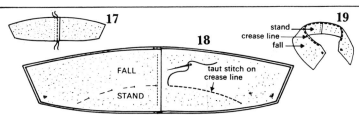

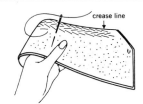

17. *Joining under collar canvas along the center back* **18.** *Sewing canvas to under collar along crease line* **19.** *The stand and fall of the collar*

20. *Pad stitching the canvas to the under collar on the fall*

21. *Pad stitching the canvas to the under collar on the stand*

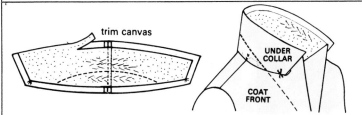

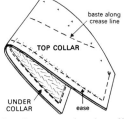

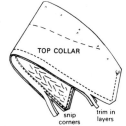

25. *Trimming the canvas on the under collar*   **26.** *Checking the fit of the under collar*

27. *Basting top and under collars together*

28. *Stitched collar seams ready for turning*

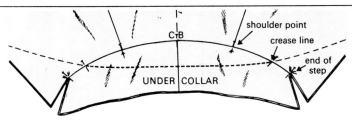

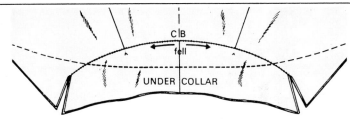

31. *Pinning the under collar to the coat neck edge*

32. *Felling the under collar to the coat neck edge*

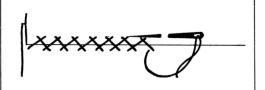

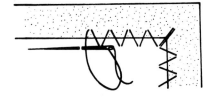

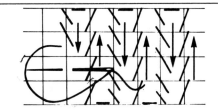

36. *Herringbone stitch*

37. *Catch stitch*

38. *Pad stitch*

and underarm seams and catch stitch as for the front (Figs. 16a and b).

Canvasing the step under collar

This type of collar should be smooth and well fitting, so great care must be taken not to distort it when stitching and pressing. Ideally, the collar should be sewn to the coat by hand to insure a perfect fit.

Sew the center back seam on the fabric, trim seam allowance to $\frac{1}{4}$ inch and press. Overlap the canvas seam (Fig. 17).

Lay the canvas to the wrong side of the undercollar with the center backs matching. Pin along the crease line, then run a taut thread along the crease line in matching thread (Fig. 18).

This crease line divides the stand and fall of the collar (Fig. 19).

With the canvas side up, pad stitch the fall and stand in lines of staggered pad stitching. Hold the work as shown in Figs. 20 and 21, so that the crease line is away from you.

Pressing the collar pieces

To fit the coat correctly, the under and top collar need to be pressed and molded before being stitched together. Lay the under collar, right side down, on an ironing board. Using a damp cloth, press the fall, gently pulling the outer edge of the collar slightly just above the shoulder position. Always pull toward the center back as this must not be stretched. Do not stretch for more than $\frac{1}{2}$ inch (Figs. 22a and b). Repeat for the stand.

Turn right side up and lay it flat with the stand folded over on the crease line. Using a damp cloth, press firmly without stretching (Fig. 23).

While the under collar is still damp curve it around a bowl, with the stand turned in, to dry in a curve (Fig. 24).

Prepare the top collar similarly, but turning the stand under to the wrong side.

Making the collar

Trim the canvas to inside the fabric seam line and check that the under collar fits the coat (Figs. 25 and 26). Place the two collar pieces right sides together and baste along the crease line. Baste on outside and step edges. There should be a slight ease on the outside edge to allow the seam to lie on the underside of the finished collar (Fig. 27).

Machine stitch, layer the seams and snip the corners (Fig. 28).

Turn the collar to the right side and work the corners or curves into a good shape. Working on the underside, baste along the stitched edges, keeping the seam rolled to the underside. Side stitch the seam edges to keep them in place (Fig. 29).

Turn under the seam allowance on the neck edge of the under collar and baste. Snip into the neck edge seam allowance of the top collar at the shoulder points. Turn under the seam allowance from the front edges to the shoulder point as shown and baste (Fig. 30).

Press very carefully without destroying

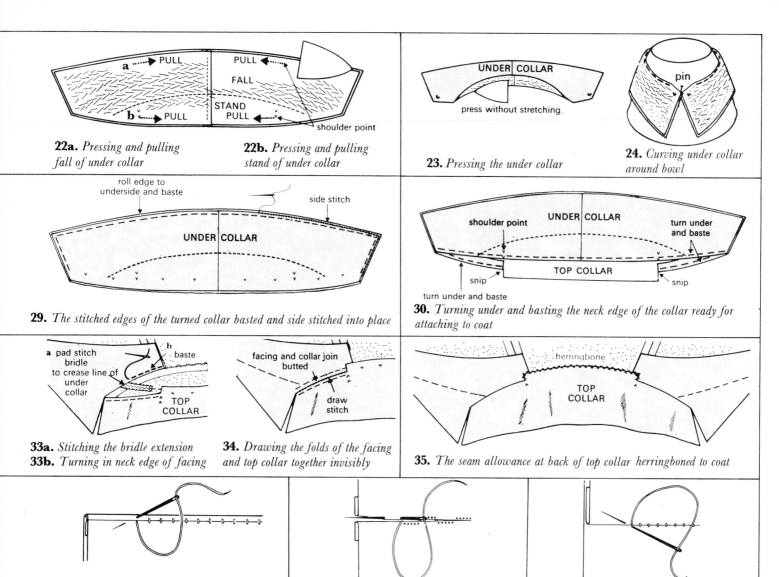

22a. *Pressing and pulling fall of under collar*

22b. *Pressing and pulling stand of under collar*

23. *Pressing the under collar*

24. *Curving under collar around bowl*

29. *The stitched edges of the turned collar basted and side stitched into place*

30. *Turning under and basting the neck edge of the collar ready for attaching to coat*

33a. *Stitching the bridle extension*
33b. *Turning in neck edge of facing*

34. *Drawing the folds of the facing and top collar together invisibly*

35. *The seam allowance at back of top collar herringboned to coat*

39. *Side stitch*

40. *Draw stitch*

41. *Felling*

the crease line.

Attaching the collar to the coat

Lay the coat, right side up, over the knees with the neck line toward you. Lay the under collar to the neck edge of the coat, right side up, with the folded edge of the under collar meeting the sewing line of the coat neck edge. Carefully match the center backs, shoulder points and crease line. Pin along the neck edge distributing the ease evenly (Fig. 31).

Fell the collar to the coat, starting at the center back and working to each end to keep the collar "sitting" centrally. Finish the ends very securely (Fig. 32).

Still with the coat over your knees, turn it over to the wrong side. Pad stitch the end of the bridle firmly to the under collar crease line (Fig. 33a). Turn in the seam allowance of the facings along the neck edge in a smooth line and baste to the coat (Fig. 33b).

Put the folded edges of the top collar to the folds of the facing. Using a draw stitch, draw the folds together making the stitches invisible (Fig. 34). The raw edge is herringboned down and eventually covered by the lining (Fig. 35). Press carefully over a tailor's ham.

Herringbone

This stitch is similar to catch stitch and is used in hems or areas where the edges need to be held down flat (Fig. 36).

Catch stitch

This is used to catch one fabric to another where bulk is to be avoided. Lift one thread of fabric with each stitch so as to be invisible on the right side. Do not pull the stitches tight (Fig. 37).

Pad stitching

Work the stitch as shown, the needle to be at right angles to the stitching line. Work with an imaginary grid, coming down one line and going up the next, without turning the work. Stagger the lines to prevent pleats being formed. Use small stitches $\frac{1}{4}$ to $\frac{1}{2}$ inch long (Fig. 38).

Side stitch

This is used to flatten edges of lapels and collars. Make a tiny stitch at right angles to the line of stitching. The stitches should not appear on the right side of the garment (Fig. 39).

Draw stitch

This stitch is used to close two folds of fabric together. Slip the needle through the top fold for $\frac{1}{4}$ inch, then directly under the end of the first stitch slip the needle through the lower fold for $\frac{1}{4}$ inch (Fig. 40).

Felling

This is a firm form of hemming, with a stitch at right angles to the hem or fold (Fig. 41).

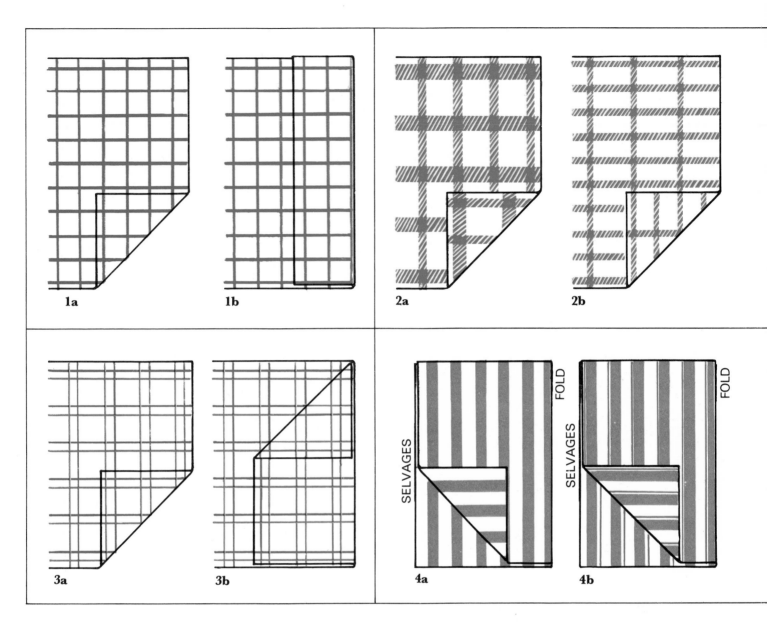

1a 1b 2a 2b

3a 3b 4a 4b

Plaids, checks and stripes

When using plaid, check or stripe fabrics, the aim is to achieve a balanced, harmonious effect in proportion to the figure. Vertical lines tend to lengthen a figure and horizontal lines have a broadening effect, but, bearing this in mind, very pleasing results can be achieved when using modern fabric designs and fashion styles. When choosing a pattern for these fabrics, give careful attention to the layout of the pattern pieces. Once this is done, the actual construction of the garment should be straightforward.

Plaids

Plaids are made from stripes crossing each other at right angles, spaced as the designer desires and repeated to form a length of fabric. In all plaids the main outlines of the design are formed by two dominant stripes, one vertical and one horizontal.

In even plaids these stripes form perfect squares, and when any square is folded diagonally or vertically in half, it forms a mirror image of itself (Figs. 1a and b). Even plaids are easy to use and ideal for those using these designs for the first time. In uneven plaids the stripes and designs can be different either lengthwise or crosswise or in both directions (Figs. 2a and b). It is not always easy to see if a plaid is a true square or not. To check this, fold the fabric diagonally through the center of the repeat, then horizontally or vertically as a double check, because some plaids have a subtle repeat which matches diagonally but not in other directions (Figs. 3a and b).

Checks

These are made in the same way as plaids and most are formed from complete squares. Some checks are oblongs, however, so fold the fabric as shown in the figure above to check their shape and accuracy.

Stripes

Stripes can be even or unevenly balanced and of varying widths. Fold across the true bias to see this clearly (Figs. 4a and b).

Striped fabrics can often be cut to create exciting visual effects; they can be used as bias bindings for pockets and cuffs, or to give a chevron effect when cut on the bias and seamed centrally.

The best and most accurate of all plaids, checks and striped fabrics are those which have the designs woven into them.

When working with printed fabrics it is essential to test the pattern as shown (Figs. 1a–4b), and also to make sure that the designs are printed in line with

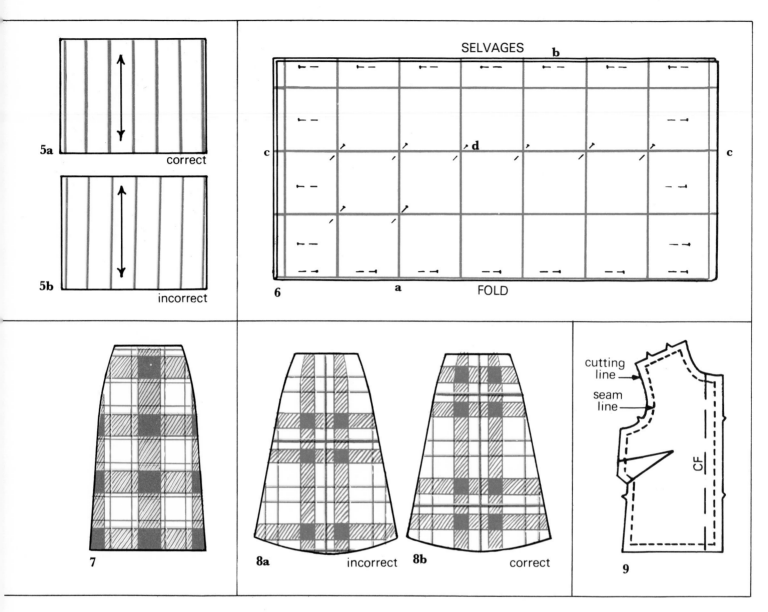

5a correct

5b incorrect

SELVAGES b

c   d   c

6   a   FOLD

7

8a incorrect   8b correct

cutting line

seam line

CF

9

the grain (Figs. 5a and b).

To find the dominant line or lines, half close the eyes and squint at the fabric, to blur the design and allow these lines to become obvious. Because a small piece of fabric does not always show a complete repeat of a design, it is best to buy from a roll and to allow extra for matching. The amount will depend on the size of the design, but $\frac{1}{4}$ yard extra for small designs and $\frac{1}{2}$ yard for large ones should be sufficient.

Styles to consider

Stripe or plaid fabrics can be used to make a whole garment, or as a contrast. Study patterns to see how the designers drew their ideas and imagine how individual touches could be added. It is a good idea to take a tracing of the garment, and to add these touches to it to see if they are suitable.

Always make sure that the pattern used is designed for plaids, checks or stripes. If it has been found that seam lines cannot be matched owing to differing angles

or style lines, then this information will be given on the pattern envelope.

Preparation of fabric

This is most important as the underneath piece of the folded fabric must exactly match the top piece.

Pin down the fold, having decided where this is to be after reference to the pattern, i.e. which part of the design is to be at the center back or center front, making sure that the fold is either at the center of a design or on a dominant line (Fig. 6a).

Pin along the selvage, matching the design every 2 inches (Fig. 6b), and across the ends of the fabric, matching the design (Fig. 6c).

Pin at intervals all over the fabric, checking underneath to see that the pattern matches exactly (Fig. 6d).

If the fabric has to be refolded to cut specific pattern pieces, this process should be repeated every time. Even with quite small checks, this procedure should be followed.

Layout

Because a great deal of time and thought has to be given to the layout of the pattern, it is essential that the pattern should fit the figure. Pin it together along the seam lines, try it on and make any necessary alterations.

Consider the following points before starting the layout:

For a straight hemline, the dominant stripe should be at the hem (Fig. 7).

For a curved hemline the dominant stripe should be above the hemline to avoid the impression it is falling out of the skirt (Figs. 8a and b).

The dominant line should not fall across the widest part of the garment, i.e. at bust or hips.

Always remember to match seam lines, not cutting lines. If this is found to be difficult then cut the pattern along the seam lines, but remember the seam allowance when cutting out the pattern pieces (Fig. 9).

For even designs, match the pattern at the following points:

2302

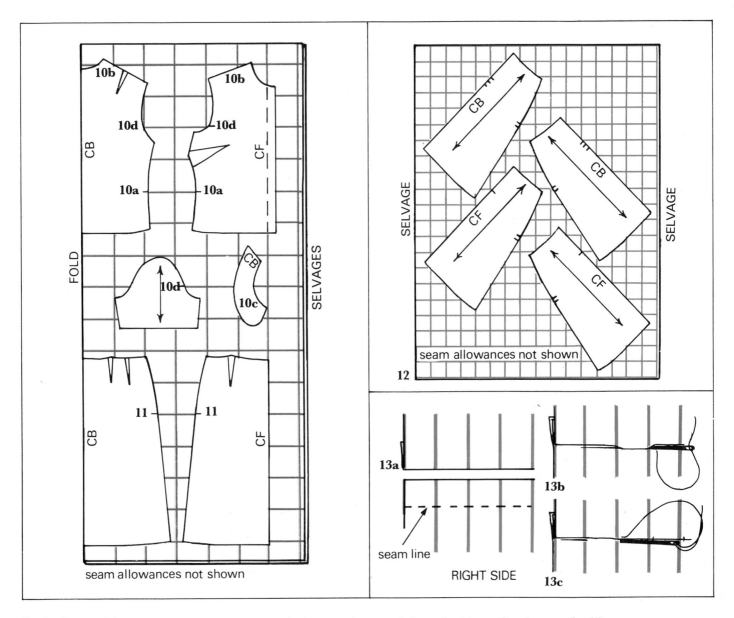

On bodice or blouse
Side seam notches. If there is an underarm dart or style line it is impossible to match the complete side seam, so use the notches so that the part that shows in wear is correct (Fig. 10a).
Shoulder seams. These are difficult to match because of the dart or ease that is sometimes included in the back shoulder line (Fig. 10b).
Center back of collar to back bodice. This should be planned carefully so that there is a horizontal as well as a vertical match. Cutting the top collar can be left until the bodice is assembled because it can then be seen whether it is better to match up the pattern at the center front rather than the back. Cutting the top collar with the center back on the bias (with a seam), can sometimes solve a difficult matching problem (Fig. 10c).
Sewing in sleeves. Match the front sleeve head notch to the front bodice armhole notch. Because of the ease at the sleeve head it is impossible to

match the complete armhole and with large plaids it is also impossible to match the pattern at the back (Fig. 10d).
For kimono or raglan sleeves, match below sleeve notches at shoulder point.

On skirts
Match the center front, center back and hem lines. Side seams can only match vertically where the slant on both is the same (Fig. 11).

On dresses
Match the full length of the centers front and back and at the hemlines.

On suits
Match the centers of the jacket to the skirt and the jacket hemline to the point where it overlaps the skirt.

On pants
Work from the side seam notches, making sure that the hemline matches at the side seam points.

Cutting on the bias
Very pleasing effects can be obtained by cutting the fabric on the bias. To do this, cut each piece singly, matching carefully each time. Remember to reverse the pattern piece for the second piece of a pair (Fig. 12).
Uneven plaids are more difficult and cannot be matched in both directions. Choose the design that is to be emphasized both vertically and horizontally and match this for the centers and hemline.

Slip basting
This method of basting is the easiest way in which to match the designs accurately.
Lay two pieces side by side, right side up. Turn under the seam allowance on one piece (Fig. 13a).
Lay the folded edge along the sewing line of the other piece (Fig. 13b).
Take a stitch through the fold (Fig. 13c).
Pick up the under piece exactly on the sewing line (Fig. 13d).

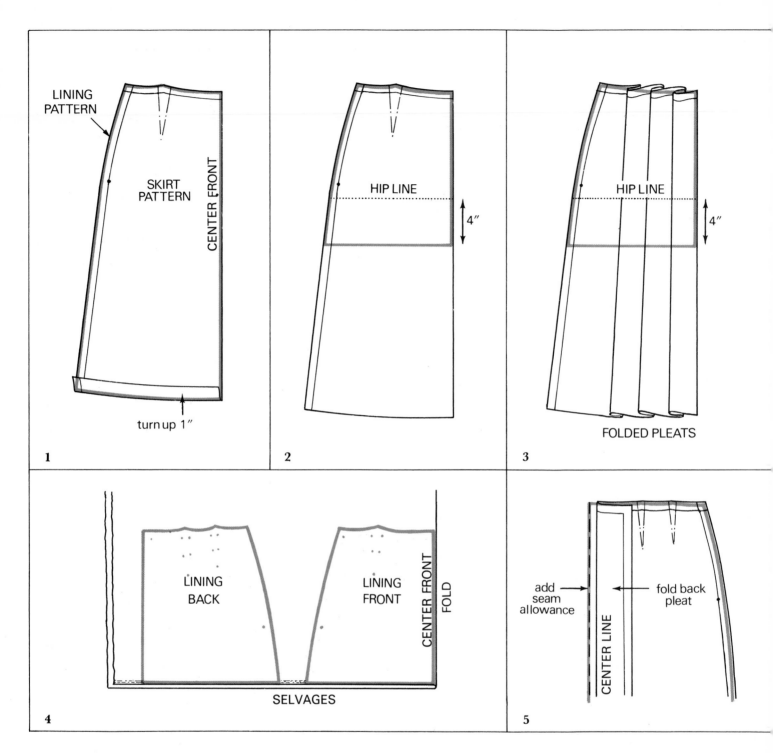

1

LINING PATTERN

SKIRT PATTERN

CENTER FRONT

turn up 1″

2

HIP LINE

4″

3

HIP LINE

4″

FOLDED PLEATS

4

LINING BACK

LINING FRONT

CENTER FRONT

FOLD

SELVAGES

5

add seam allowance

fold back pleat

CENTER LINE

ADVANCED DRESSMAKING

Lining and re-lining a skirt

A lining prolongs the life of a skirt by covering the seaming and protecting the fabric from wear and tear. In addition the lining prevents the skirt from stretching, helps to preserve its shape, reduces wrinkling and adds body to limp fabrics.

If a lining is not to affect the fit or appearance of the skirt it must always be lighter in weight and softer than the skirt fabric.

The choice of lining material also depends on how the skirt fabric is to be cleaned; whether it is to be washed by hand or machine, whether it will need ironing or whether it must be dry cleaned. The lining must have similar characteristics. So check the labels for washing instructions when buying and, if in doubt, ask for advice.

Lining variations

The lining shape depends on the style

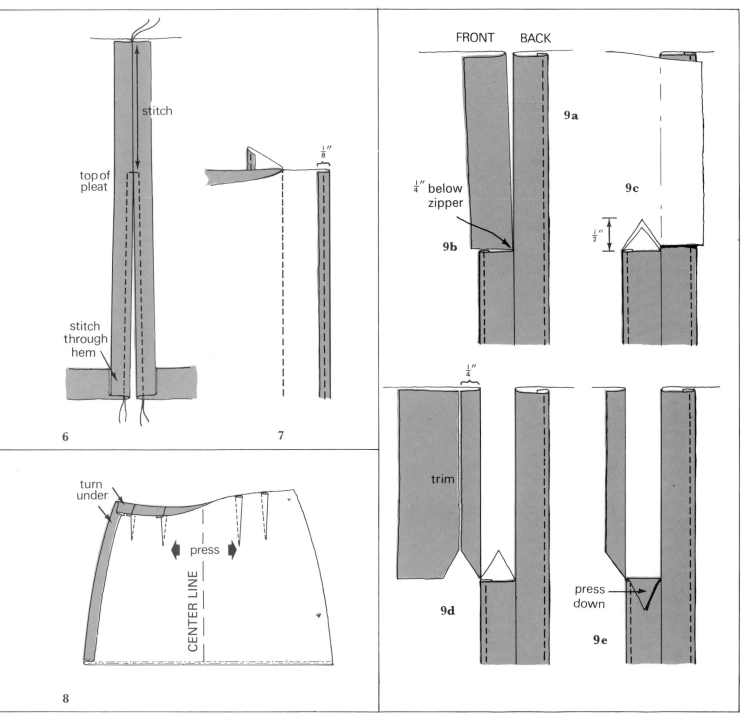

FRONT **BACK**

9a

¼" below zipper

9b

9c

½"

¼"

trim

9d

press down

9e

6

stitch

top of pleat

stitch through hem

7

⅛"

8

turn under

press

CENTER LINE

of the skirt. For a simple straight or "A" line skirt, the lining can be either full length or half length, falling just below the hip line. Or, the skirt can be lined on the front or back only. For a skirt with a single pleat the lining should have a slit, and for a pleated skirt the best version is a half length smooth lining as for the simple or "A" line skirts.

Cutting the lining

For a full length lining use the original pattern pieces, cutting them 1 inch shorter than for the skirt (Fig. 1). For a half length lining on a plain skirt, cut 4 inches below the hip line (Fig. 2). For a half length lining on a pleated

skirt, fold the pleats in the paper pattern and cut the lining from this to 4 inches below the hips (Fig. 3).

For lining the front or back only, cut the appropriate pieces as for a half length lining (Fig. 2).

When making a half length lining place the pattern piece on the lining fabric so that the lower edge is to the selvage, thus avoiding the bulk caused by a hem (Fig. 4).

For a single pleat, omit the extension but be sure to leave a seam allowance (Fig. 5).

If an old skirt is to be relined, remove the old lining carefully, rip the seams and darts, press the pieces carefully and use as the pattern.

Making the lining

All full linings are made in exactly the same way as the skirt itself, leaving the zipper opening ¼ inch longer than for the skirt. Remember to position the zipper opening at the right side for a left side opening.

For single pleats, sew to the top of the pleat and make neat the opening with a narrow hem (Fig. 6).

Because lining fabrics tend to fray, make neat the seams by turning under ⅛ inch of the seam allowance and top-stitch (Fig. 7).

For a single piece of lining sew the darts and press under the seam and waist allowances (Fig. 8).

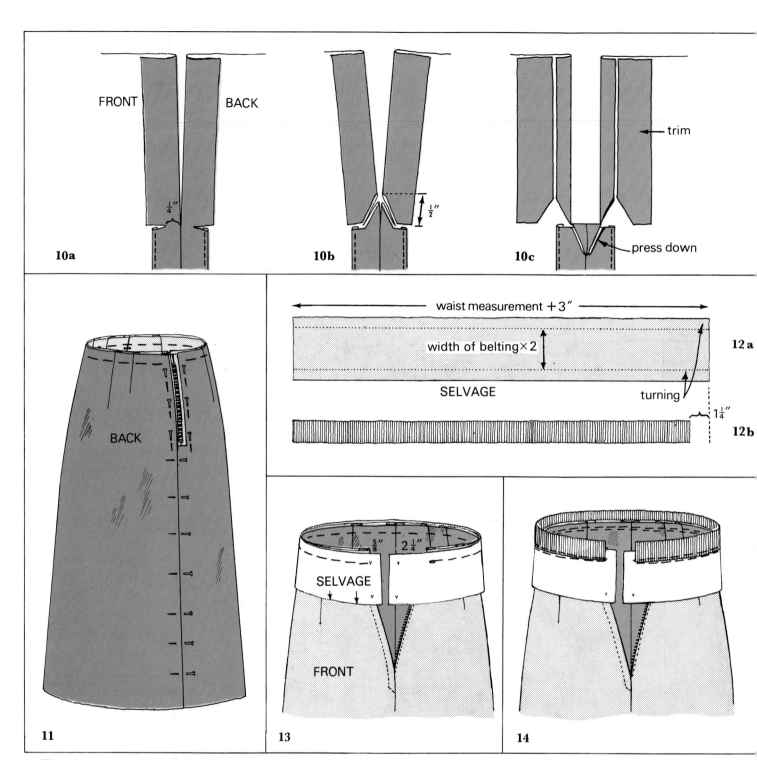

10a FRONT BACK $\frac{1}{4}''$

10b $\frac{1}{2}''$

10c trim press down

11 BACK

12a waist measurement +3" width of belting×2 SELVAGE turning

12b $1\frac{1}{4}''$

13 SELVAGE FRONT $\frac{5}{8}''$ $2\frac{1}{4}''$

14

Test the temperature of the iron on a spare piece of lining as too hot an iron distorts some man-made fibers. Press the lining carefully, making sure that the darts lie away from the back and front center lines, thus avoiding bulk under the skirt darts as shown in Fig. 8.

Making neat the zipper opening

The bottom of the seam opening on the lining can be made neat by using either of two methods, depending upon the method chosen to sew the zipper into the skirt.

Lapped or concealed zipper

Press the back seam allowance to con-tinue the seam line (Fig. 9a).
Cut straight through the seam allowance to the top of the seam (Fig. 9b).
Cut a miter in the front lining fabric $\frac{1}{2}$ inch high and $\frac{1}{2}$ inch wide (Fig. 9c).
Fold the seam allowance back to the end of the miter and trim to $\frac{1}{4}$ inch (Fig. 9d).
Fold the miter to the wrong side and press carefully (Fig. 9e).

Invisible or semi-concealed zipper

Snip both seam allowances to within $\frac{1}{4}$ inch of the seam line (Fig. 10a).
From the folded edges of the allowances cut a half miter $\frac{1}{2}$ inch high by $\frac{1}{4}$ inch wide (Fig. 10b).
Cut the allowance back to the original fold line, fold down the miters and press carefully (Fig. 10c).

Sewing the lining to the skirt

The lining can be sewn in before or after the waistband is attached. Remember that it is easier to re-line a skirt if the lining is not stitched in at the waist.
Method 1: Before the band is attached. Place the skirt and lining with wrong sides together and pin and baste along the waist. Pin down the seams and around the zipper (Fig. 11).
Place the waistband with one long edge to the selvage, if at all possible, and cut it 3 inches longer than the waist measurement and twice as wide as the belting

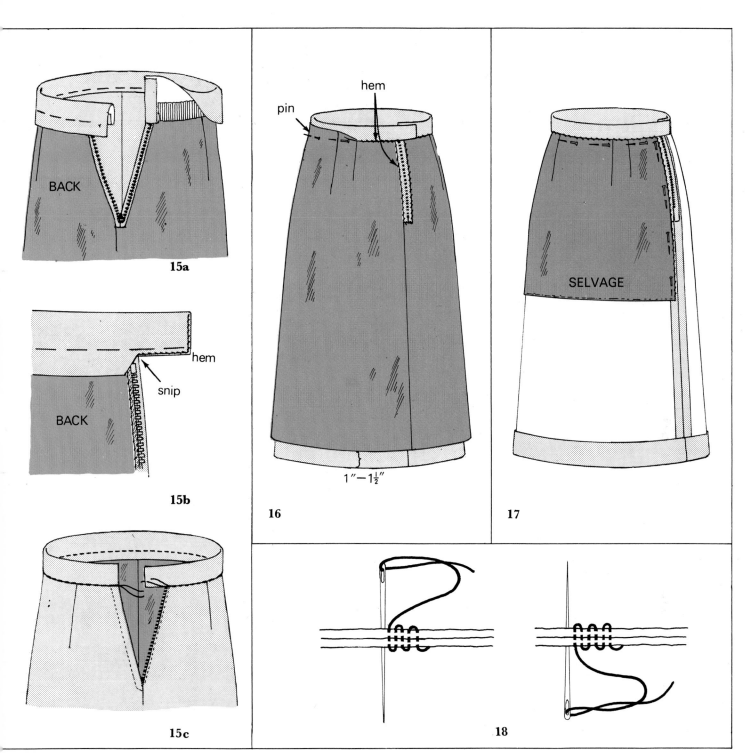

15a

15b

15c

16

17

18

ribbon, plus two turnings (Fig. 12a). Cut the belting 1¼ inches shorter than the band (Fig. 12b).

Ease the skirt onto the long cut edge of the waistband leaving ⅝ inch overlap at the front zipper edge and 2⅜ inches at the back. Baste through band, skirt and lining and stitch (Fig. 13).

Sew the belting just above this line, placing it so that there is a ⅝ inch turning left at both ends (Fig. 14).

Turn in the seam allowance at the ends of the belting and fold the band over the belting along the waistline (Fig. 15a).

Snip at the zipper and turn under along the extension and baste along the length of the band. Hem the extension and the front ends (Fig. 15b).

Machine or stab stitch along the waistband seam working from the right side (Fig. 15c).

Method 2: After the waistband is sewn on. Make the skirt and attach the waistband as above.

Place the lining to the skirt with wrong sides together and pin down the seams and around the zipper (Fig. 16).

Turn under the waist seam allowance to the waistband sewing line and slipstitch all around (Fig. 16).

For all full length linings, turn up the hem 1 to 1½ inches shorter than the skirt and hem.

Method 3: Half lining either front or back. Make the skirt and attach the waistband.

Place lining to the appropriate piece of the skirt, with wrong sides together, and pin (Fig. 17).

Slipstitch down the side seams and along the waistband machine stitching line.

Stab stitch

Working from the right side, push the needle down vertically, and pull the needle through from the wrong side. Then push the needle up vertically, and pull through from the right side (Fig. 18). The stitches should be very small and evenly spaced.

2308

Rich look for a caftan

The muted color and casual style of this caftan make it the perfect setting for a touch of vivid embroidery at neck and sleeve. The stitchery lends texture and interest to an otherwise simple garment and it is adaptable enough to use on other styles too.

To work the embroidery

Materials required for the embroidery at the neck, front opening and sleeve hems:

☐ D.M.C. 6-strand Floss in the following quantities and colors: 1 skein each 961 rose pink, 815 raspberry; 3 skeins 781 amber gold; 4 skeins 3371 coffee

☐ D.M.C. Tapestry Yarn in the following quantity and color: 1 skein 7947 flame

☐ 1 package bronze glass beads

☐ beading needle

☐ Coats and Clark's crewel needles, Nos. 6 and 7

☐ Coats and Clark's chenille needle, No.18

Method of working

Ideally the embroidery should be worked on the fabric before assembling the garment. The tracing patterns (Figs. 1, 2) give the design for the front of the caftan and the design used for the sleeves. The broken line in Fig. 1 indicates the seam line at the neck and front opening of the illustrated caftan. This can, of course, be altered or adjusted as the style of the garment requires.

Trace Fig. 1 as given onto the right front of the caftan; then trace the design once more one half inch below, omitting the detail at the neck edge. Repeat this procedure in reverse onto the left front. Trace Fig. 2 as given the required number of times around the lower edge of each sleeve, as shown in the photograph.

Fig. 2 Tracing pattern for the embroidery at sleeve hems

Fig. 1 Tracing pattern for the embroidery at neck and front opening

Follow Fig. 3 to work the embroidery. The key indicates the color and stitch used in each area. All areas which correspond to the numbered areas are worked in the same color and stitch.

Use three strands of floss in the needle for working satin stitch and four strands for working the rest of the embroidery. Use crewel needles Nos. 6 and 7 for working with four and three strands respectively. When working with tapestry yarn, use a chenille needle.

A detail of the embroidery at the front opening

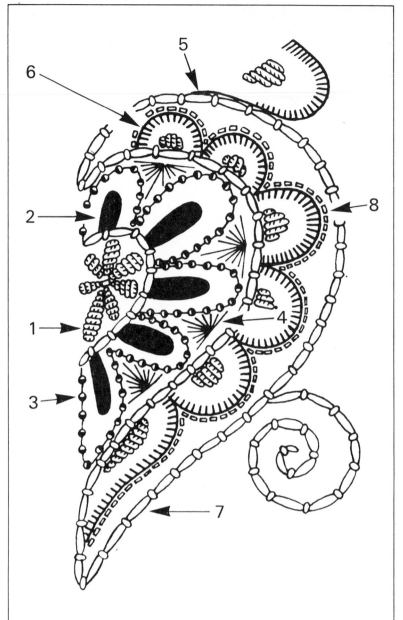

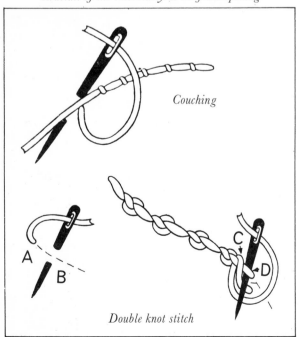

Couching

Double knot stitch

Color and stitch key

1	– 781	} satin stitch
2	– 3371	
3	– 961	– double knot stitch
4	– 815	– straight stitch
5	– 3371	– stem stitch
6	– 3371	– buttonhole stitch
(T) 7	– 7947	– couching
8	– bronze beads	
T	– tapestry yarn	

Fig. 3 The working chart indicates placement of stitches and colors. The numbered key gives shades of floss and tapestry yarn